Captured M across the Hillforts of Cheshire

Compiled by
David Joyce and Barbara Foxwell

For the Habitats and Hillforts Landscape
Partnership Scheme
Cheshire West and Chester

First Edition

Copyright © Cheshire West and Chester 2011

Contents

i-ii	**Preface**
iii	**Introduction**
iv-vi	**Overview of the Landscape Character of the Sandstone Ridge**
vii-x	**Overview of the Archaeology Background**
xi-xii	**LIDAR - Peeling away history**

1-26 **Helsby**
- 2-8   Helsby on the hill
- 9-10   Memories of Barbara Foxwell
- 10-12   Memories of the Helsby Tuesday Club
- 13-15   Helsby Golf Club
- 16-18   Climbing at Helsby and Frodsham
- 18-19   Trig Point
- 19-22   Wartime Observation Post
- 22-25   Cold War Bunker

27-42 **Woodhouse Hill**
- 29-31   The Hamlet of Woodhouses
- 32-33   Around the Hillfort
- 33-34   Dunsdale Hollow
- 34-35   Frodsham Golf Club
- 35-36   Foxhill
- 36   Woodland Trust
- 36-37   Sand Caves
- 37-39   Queen Charlotte's Wood Campsite
- 39-41   Mersey View Pleasure Grounds and The Forest Hills Hotel

43-56 **Eddisbury**
- 44-47   The View from the Top
- 47-49   Delamere School
- 50   William J Varley
- 51-52   The Chamber in the Forest
- 52-53   Wartime Activities

54	Local Farms and Houses
54-55	Marl Pits

57-76 Kelsborrow Castle

59-60	The Early History of Castle Hill
60-64	Kelsborrow Estate
64-70	The Hardy Family
70-71	Kelsall Transmitter Tower
71-73	Local Memories
73-74	Riddles in the Cliffs
74	Willington Fruit Farm

77-88 Beeston Castle

78-80	Beeston Crags
81-82	Archaeological Excavations
82-83	Motorcycle Hill Climbs
83-84	The Treasure Seekers
84-85	Operation Dodo
85-86	Village Fetes
86-87	Entertainments and Historical Re-enactments
87	Darker Moments
87-88	Climbing

89-104 Maiden Castle

90-92	Renewed Heathland
93-95	Around the Hillfort
95-96	The Sandstone Trail Race
96	A Quiet Place?
97-98	Military Involvement
98	Kitty's Stone
99	Caves
99-100	Water Supplies
100-102	Interviews by Vanessa Nuttall

105-107 Final Thoughts
108 Other Publications

Captured Memories across the Hillforts of Cheshire

Preface

Habitats & Hillforts is a 3-year Heritage Lottery Funded project focusing on the prominent Sandstone Ridge extending 30 km from Frodsham to Bickerton. This ridge has had a major historical impact on the culture, social and environmental history of this rural part of mid-Cheshire, and contains archaeological sites of major significance — including a chain of six Iron Age hillfort sites at Helsby, Woodhouse, Eddisbury, Kelsborrow, Beeston and Maiden Castle.

The scheme is supported by the Heritage Lottery Fund and is a partnership of local organisations and residents working together to improve the hillforts and surrounding habitats; to enhance access and interpretation, and provide opportunities for volunteering and training.

At the beginning of the scheme, two local volunteers were approached to develop a local history project about the living history of the Sandstone Ridge and particularly the special Iron Age hillforts that are situated along it. David Joyce and Barbara Foxwell were pleased to take up the challenge and embarked on collating 'Captured Memories'. We collectively felt it was important to capture local people's memories about this interesting landscape and how people used and enjoyed it over the past 100 years.

I would like to take this opportunity to thank David and Barbara for their hard work in creating 'Captured Memories'. It has been a real strength of the scheme and they have been flying the flag amongst many local groups and societies to gather this information.

We hope you enjoy reading this booklet. There are audio podcasts available for listening on the Habitats and Hillforts website as well as an area where you can add your memories at:-

www.habitatsandhillforts.co.uk

Ellie Soper, Habitats and Hillforts Project Manager

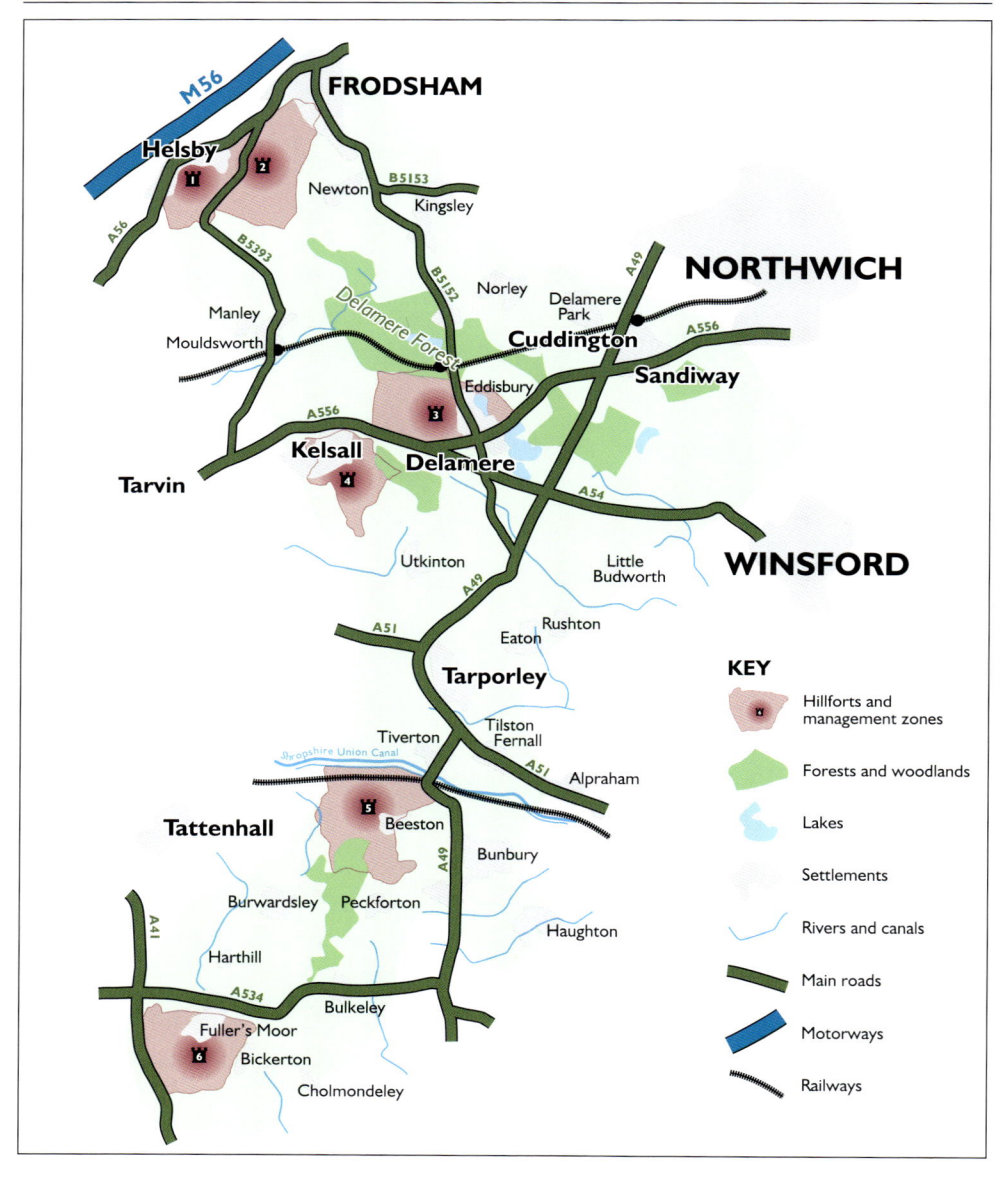

Captured Memories across the Hillforts of Cheshire

1. Helsby Hillfort
2. Woodhouse Hillfort
3. Eddisbury Hillfort
4. Kelsborrow Castle
5. Beeston Castle
6. Maiden Castle

Captured Memories across the Hillforts of Cheshire

Introduction

The Iron Age Hillforts of Cheshire have acted as a focal point for so many activities for hundreds of years. Their dominant positions have drawn people for generations to work, play or simply sit and stare, but little of this has been recorded.

So much of our history is lost. We may know about the big events but it is also our everyday activities that shape our society and these are, all too often, forgotten. As part of the Habitats and Hillforts Landscape Partnership Schme we have tried to capture some of those memories.

Our objective has been to collect information on activities that have taken place in the immediate vicinity of the hillforts in relatively recent times. We are not historians and our decisions as to what to include are totally arbitrary. The key has been; does the information interest, amuse or inform us. We hope you agree with our choices. We have shamelessly plagiarised other publications but have always tried to identify our sources. We strongly recommend that you follow up on some of these documents as they contain a wealth of other information on the local, social history of the area. We have talked to residents and scanned publications but have accepted the information at face value. This booklet is a snapshot of what we found during 2009 – 2011. We leave it to others to judge and verify the facts presented. In order to keep the flavour of the sources of information we collected, there has been no attempt to convert imperial to metric measurements.

There are too many people that have helped us for us to be able to acknowledge and list them individually. We are sure that if we tried we would forget somebody vital. We are truly grateful for all the help we have been given. Please accept our sincere thanks. Wherever possible we have identified individuals in the text or referenced our sources.

David Joyce and Barbara Foxwell

Captured Memories across the Hillforts of Cheshire

Overview of the Landscape Character of the Sandstone Ridge

The six hillforts that are the subject of this booklet are all situated along the Sandstone Ridge which acts as the backbone of Cheshire. Colin Slater, Ecology Project Officer for Habitats and Hillforts, provided an overview of this spectacular landscape.

The ridge stands prominently above the surrounding plain and is visually one of the most distinctive landmarks in the Cheshire landscape. It runs roughly north-south from Helsby through Tarporley and on to Duckington for some 30 km, emerging and dropping back down into the plain as a series of scarps and sandstone outcrops. The ridge has a very strong cultural and natural character, for example there is a concentration of prehistoric features, woodland and heathland, sandstone quarries and exposures and sandstone buildings, walls and sunken lanes.

Looking north along the ridge from Bickerton Hill

Due to the localised ridge and valley features of the undulating topography and a wide variation in woodland cover, this landscape exhibits varying degrees of enclosure and contrasting scales. At many locations, solid blocks of woodland (including conifers) and high hedgerows combine to provide strong enclosure, creating an impression of a small-scale verdant landscape. The sense of enclosure by lush, dense vegetation is further reinforced when travelling along sunken roads between high hedges or valley bottoms below wooded ridge lines. Elsewhere, reduced tree cover leads to a more open landscape with a dominant hedgerow pattern, particularly evident from many elevated positions available along the network of narrow lanes. Expansive, long distance views provide an important element of this landscape type as they are widely available from the higher ground and contribute significantly to the distinctive character of the landscape. These vary between narrow views framed by high vegetation to spectacular panoramic views from open vantage points. Views extend over the surrounding plain as far as the Welsh hills in the west and the Peak District in the east. Locations at the northern and southern ends of the ridge enjoy views of the Mersey Valley and the Shropshire Hills respectively.

This elevated ridge has a height of between 100 and 212m above sea level. The underlying bedrock comprises Helsby sandstone and Tarporley siltstone with a small amount of glacial till in occasional places. Outcrops of Triassic sandstone show cross-bedding of the layers indicating that the rocks were formed originally as windblown sand dunes. The Sandstone Ridge is generally overlain by free-draining brown earths and brown sands. The steep slopes and thin acid soils support concentrations of woodland, some ancient oakwood, but much of vegetation is of more recent, secondary origin or has been planted with conifers. Bird species are well represented, with several uncommon breeding species attracted to the elevated position, extensive woodlands and deadwood habitat, for example, buzzard, sparrowhawk, raven and pied flycatcher.

Heathland is also characteristic and remains most intact from agricultural improvement on Bickerton Hill. Heathland was once a common sight in Cheshire, but has become increasingly fragmented and denuded. A number of woodlands are listed as Sites of Biological Importance (SBI) such as Peckforton Woods, and there are Sites of Special Scientific Interest (SSSI) at Peckforton, Bickerton and Raw Head. The last site is of national importance for its sandstone exposures. A number of other geological and geomorphological features are of regional importance.

Pasture dominates the land use and is enclosed by hawthorn hedgerows and sandstone walls in the south. Arable cultivation of fodder crops and potatoes plus orchards and fruit farming are located on the better draining, gentler slopes of the ridge. Settlement along the ridge is mainly small scale and dispersed and comprises individual farms and houses. There are areas of modern development, which have changed the settlement pattern, such as at Utkinton and Quarry Bank but there is only one large urban settlement which is the modern village of Kelsall to the west, which grew from a dispersed pattern into a nucleated centre in the 20th century.

The northern areas lay within the extensive former Royal Forest of Mara (Delamere) and this medieval forest covered a vast portion of Cheshire. During the medieval period it became increasingly common for hunting to take place in deer parks and there are two former sites on the ridge which are identified by the place names Old Pale and New Pale. The enclosure of the forest was finally completed in 1819. Agricultural land was enclosed, creating the pattern of small to medium (up to 8ha) regular fields with straight hawthorn hedgerows. In the southern areas enclosure and forestry were also occurring, but on a significantly smaller scale. These areas were also subject to significant change by the activities of the local estates to improve their agricultural land.

Evidence of former industries is visible in the landscape, with numerous small sandstone quarries and copper mining in the south. Quarried sandstone from the ridge has been used extensively in the construction of local buildings and boundary walls, adding a distinctive architecture and colour to the area. There are a number of high status residences on the ridge including the brick c 1700 Utkinton Hall, the 19th century castle at Peckforton (grade I) and the pebble-dashed 20th century Tirley Garth.

Overview of the Archaeological Background

Dan Garner, Archaeology Project Officer for Habitats and Hillforts, provided this overview of the ancient history of the sites.

The focus of the Habitats and Hillforts project is six Scheduled Ancient Monuments sited along the mid-Cheshire Ridge which are classified as prehistoric hilltop enclosures or 'hillforts'. These monuments are so much more than this simple classification implies, each having a long and complex history which we are only just beginning to understand.

The Ridge itself seems to have been occupied intermittently by groups of prehistoric hunter-gatherers from the early Mesolithic (10,000 to 4000 BC). These people have left very little trace in the archaeological record because they did not live in permanent settlements but had a migratory lifestyle which was spent moving between seasonal camps spread over a wide geographical area. The temporary dwellings in these camps were probably huts made of branches and reeds or wigwams with timber frames and hide coverings; so, often all that is left for the archaeologist to find are the traces of hearths in shallow pits surrounded by scatters of domestic rubbish (often the debris from the manufacture of flint tools). Stray finds of flint tools dating to the Mesolithic have been found in proximity to several of our hillfort sites but the most noteworthy finds are two possible camps. The first of these was on the western side of Harrol Edge (Frodsham) and faced towards Woodhouse hillfort; the debris from this site consisted of hundreds of fragments of debitage, or waste, from the manufacture of flint blades or microliths which are a signature tool of the Mesolithic. The second site produced a similar assemblage of material but was focused on a rock shelter at Carden Park to the south of Maiden Castle (Bickerton Hill). We cannot infer that the sites of the later hillforts had any particular importance/significance for these early migratory peoples but the hilltops themselves may have performed a practical function in terms of tracking herds of game or as distinctive landmarks to guide their movement through the landscape.

The start of the Neolithic (4000 to 2500 BC) is characterised in Britain by a shift towards farming: the growing of crops; the keeping of animals and the building of permanent settlements. In some parts of Britain these early farmers began to enclose particular hilltops using a broken system of banks and ditches known as 'causewayed enclosures'. Their precise function is uncertain but they may have been intended as defended camps, seasonal fairs/tribal gathering places, places for the disposal of the dead or corrals for annual round-ups of cattle and livestock.

Captured Memories across the Hillforts of Cheshire

Neolithic artefacts in the form of leaf-shaped arrowheads and polished stone axe heads have been recovered as stray finds in the vicinity of several of our hillforts including Woodhouse, Eddisbury, Peckforton and Beeston. It would be misleading to suggest that these artefacts alone indicate that 'causewayed enclosures' lie beneath any of our hillforts. However, recent excavations on Helsby hill have identified the remains of several layers of burnt clay, rock and wood charcoal sealed beneath the later hillfort rampart which have been dated to about 3,900 BC. Furthermore, at Beeston Castle archaeological excavation has identified a number of pits and postholes which were dated to the Neolithic and possibly indicated enclosure of the hill at this time. These features and stray finds offer tantalising hints about the early significance of the hilltops on which our hillforts were later built.

Many of our hillforts have also produced evidence of Early to Middle Bronze Age (2500 to 1500 BC) activity on the hilltops; in the main this has taken the form of a distinctive flint artefact type known as a 'barbed and tanged arrowhead'. However, pottery urns containing human cremated bone have also been identified at both Eddisbury and Beeston. It is possible that these urns had originally been buried beneath circular burial mounds or barrows which were a common method of honouring the dead during the Bronze Age. Recent excavations at Eddisbury have also recovered a sandstone boulder decorated with a series of 'cup marks' often considered to be a form of Bronze Age rock art. This boulder is a complete object and may well have served as a marker for a burial somewhere on the hilltop. Perhaps this suggests that the hilltops were mainly associated with human burial and ritual practices at this time.

Bronze Age Rock Art, Eddisbury

The actual process of enclosing the hilltops appears to have begun in the Middle or Late Bronze Age (1500 to 700 BC) and this was possibly intended to formally delimit the hilltops as special/significant places in the landscape. To date we have been able to demonstrate that the first ramparts to be built at Woodhouse, Helsby and Beeston belong to this period and that construction on these sites probably began between 1,200 and 700 BC. Archaeological excavation at Beeston has provided us with a greater depth of understanding about the site during the Late Bronze Age than any of the other Cheshire hillforts. The evidence includes debris from metal working in the form of crucible and mould fragments associated with the casting of bronze objects; a number of complete bronze objects have been recovered from the site including 5 socketed axe heads and a spear head. The craft of bronze casting was probably viewed as an almost magical process in the Bronze Age and the technical knowledge required would have conveyed special status to any accomplished bronze-smith. A number of large pits were also excavated and were filled with charred cereal grains which might suggest that the produce of the surrounding farm land was being stored and processed at the hillfort. Beeston also revealed structural elements to a number of Bronze Age roundhouses as well as evidence for domestic occupation in the form of pottery jars and quern stones for grinding cereals to make flour.

Excavation at Helsby, 2010

During the ensuing Early Iron Age (700 to 100 BC) these ramparts were bolstered with ever larger and more imposing banks and ditches that seem to have been intended to fortify the hilltops. The defensive nature of the Iron Age developments are most clearly demonstrated by the elaborate arrangements associated with some of our hillforts' entrances; particularly the in-turned banks and putative 'guard chambers' associated with the entrances at Eddisbury and Maiden Castle. The need for defence seems to have been associated with a specific function and this was most likely to do with the storage, protection and regulation of agricultural surplus such as grain and livestock. It is perhaps worth remembering that the Cheshire countryside would still have been home to large predators such as the brown bear, lynx and wolf at the time that our hillforts were being occupied. A form of Iron Age ceramic known as VCP (very coarse pottery) has also been recovered from some of our hillforts including Beeston and Eddisbury. This ceramic is derived from pottery containers used in the production and transport of salt crystals from the Cheshire brine fields; perhaps indicating that the hillforts had a role in the regulation of the trade in salt. Excavations at Beeston also identified a number of high status metal objects including the remains of an elaborate bronze and leather drinking cup that was perhaps used during feasts or festivals.

It is generally thought that the hillforts had fallen out of use by the Late Iron Age (100 BC to 43 AD) possibly as a result of a shift in the needs of local society. The evidence from Beeston suggests that there was a dramatic change of function and a lack of maintenance of the ramparts at this time; the latest dateable Iron Age object from the site was an iron javelin head dated 300 to 100 BC. The latest evidence we have on our other hillforts comes from excavations at Helsby which recovered charred cereal grains from the interior of the hillfort that date to between 200 and 100 BC.

Some later developments ...

Some hillforts were later occasionally re-occupied during times of stress and upheaval such as the Roman invasion of Britain in the mid 1st century AD. Interestingly, a bronze Roman coin (sestertius) dated to AD 22 was found on Helsby hill during the 1960s and it is conceivable that this coin arrived in Cheshire through trade a decade or two before the Roman military conquest began. Later evidence from both Beeston and Eddisbury includes domestic debris such as pottery and metalwork dating to the 2nd and 3rd centuries AD. This suggests that our hillforts were being occupied by Romano-British people (Romanised natives) perhaps as farmsteads during the relatively stable period of Pax Romana. After the later collapse of Roman government in Britain in the early 5th century AD the hillforts may have again come in to use as places of refuge. The evidence for this on the Cheshire hillforts is very slight at present but the ramparts at Helsby appear to have been furnished with a new internal stone retaining wall after AD 400 to 530.

Later still we have a documentary reference to Eddisbury being refortified as a royal Saxon burh by Aethelflaed 'Lady of the Mercians' in AD 914 in response to the constant threat of Viking raids from the north. Recent excavations at Eddisbury have identified a clay oven built in to the back of the inner hillfort rampart which has been dated to between 750 and 1000 AD; further dating on the outer rampart and ditch are currently awaited and further traces of the royal burh may yet come to light.

Perhaps the founding of the medieval castle at Beeston in the early AD 1220s by Ranulf 6th Earl of Chester and its later re-use during the years of the English Civil War (1642-46) can be seen as the final phase in the story of our hilltop forts. Then again maybe not, as you will learn by perusing the pages of this book.

LIDAR - Peeling away history

The Habitats and Hillforts scheme commissioned an airborne LIDAR survey of the entire Sandstone Ridge. This was done to record the area around the hillforts in more detail and to find new archaeological sites, particularly in wooded areas where other methods of survey can be difficult. The purpose of the survey is twofold.

- It allows us to look at the Hillforts and other known archaeological sites in more detail
- Future examination of this impressive survey is likely to result in the identification of previously unrecorded archaeological sites in the Sandstone Ridge.

What is LIDAR?
LIDAR stands for LIght Detection And Ranging. Airborne LIDAR is a method of laser scanning that produces 3-dimensional images of ground surface. Essentially, a plane carries a laser beam that is sent in pulses to the ground. The speed and intensity of the returning beam is measured which gives the varying heights of surface being measured. Combined with precise location data derived from a GPS (global positioning system) it is then possible to create a 3-dimensional model of the ground surface.

As the laser beams are fired from the plane overhead, they are reflected back whenever they come into contact with something. As the beam travels towards the ground if it strikes anything in passing, part of the beam is reflected back to the sensor and forms what is known as the first return.

The rest of the beam continues on towards the ground, reflecting back beams whenever it comes into contact with an object, (such as a tree) until it hits the ground or other solid surface (e.g a building). This is known as the last return.
Where there is tree cover, the beam will reflect back when it encounters the tree canopy (first return)then also travel on through significant gaps in the canopy to reach the ground surface below (last return).

This distinction in the differing reflected beams is important because LIDAR is capable of producing different types of 3D surface models.

By using the first return data a Digital Surface Model (DSM) can be created which shows the surveyed area with all the vegetation and structures.

Captured Memories across the Hillforts of Cheshire

Using only the last return data, a Digital Terrain Model (DTM) can be created which shows only the ground surface. This model of the ground can then be examined to identify archaeological features shown by variations in the ground surface e.g banks and ditches.

The LIDAR images are shown on the title page for each Hillfort Chapter.

> **Reference**
> Crutchley, S and Crow, P 2009 The Light Fantastic – Using Airborne Lidar in Archaeological survey. Swindon: English Heritage

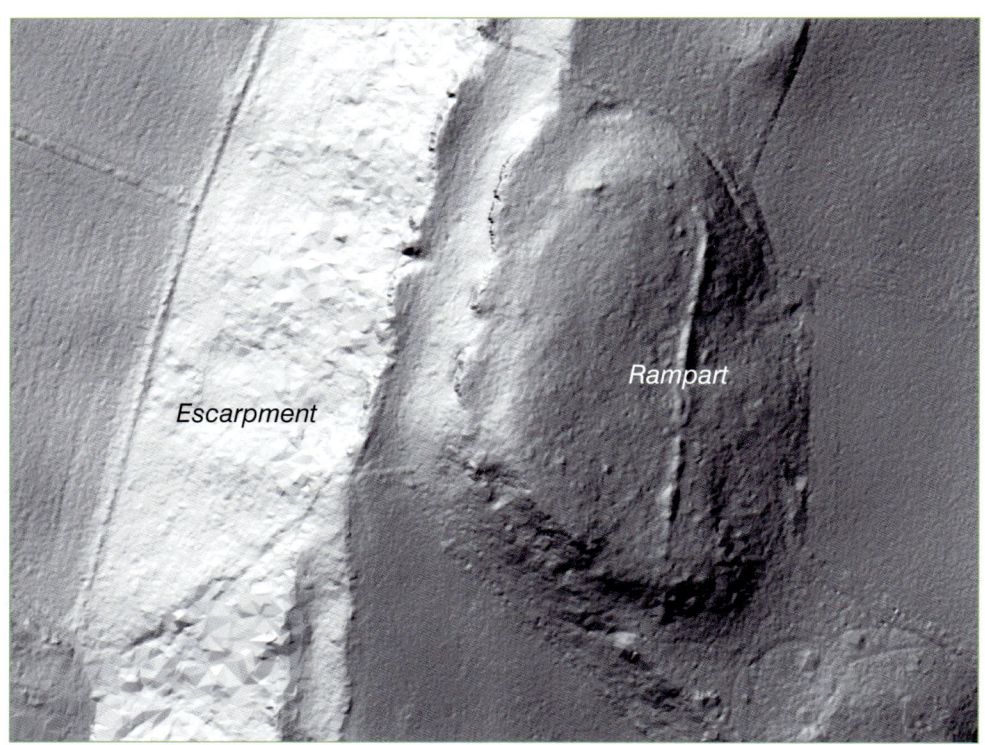

LIDAR image of Woodhouse Hillfort

Captured Memories across the Hillforts of Cheshire

Artist's impression of Helsby Hillfort by Dai Owen

View of Helsby, 2010

LIDAR view of Helsby – see page xi

HELSBY HILLFORT

Helsby and the Hill

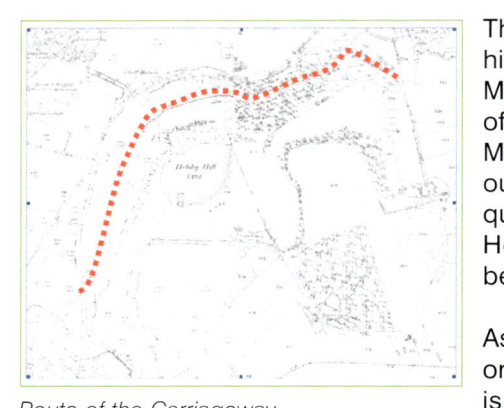

Route of the Carriageway

The starting point for many climbing to the hillfort is the Quarry car park. The Old Mountskill Quarry produced 1000's of tons of sandstone which were ferried across the Mersey from the 1830s onwards but fell out of use. Between 1988 and 1990 the quarry workings were transformed into the Helsby Quarry Woodlands Park and became a local nature reserve in 2002.

As you climb up Helsby Hill from the west or northern sides, one feature you will see is the remains of another 'road'. The line is still well defined and there are the remains of kerbing stones to be seen at some points. This carriageway was built by Samuel Burgess jnr and the Marquis of Cholmondeley between 1866 and 1870 and originally went from the Chester Road (A56) up the gulley and onwards. It was built as a leisure drive for the local gentry or as a business venture to encourage residential development by neighbouring city merchants and professional men. At that time the area was considered desirable with pure sea breeze from the nearby St George's Channel.

As you stand on Helsby Hill you are rewarded with magnificent views of Helsby and along the Mersey Valley, across to Liverpool. Further afield are the Clwydian Hills to the west and even

Where 'angels' dare to tread - Helsby Boy's Choir 1926

Panoramic view of Helsby from the Hill

HILL ROAD, HELSBY

glimpses of Beeston Castle and beyond to the south along the sandstone ridge.

Helsby Hill has been a favourite recreational site for many years. Parties came by train to Helsby station and walked up the hill to Clark's Field with their own brass and silver bands playing. On the field there were tea rooms, a tuck shop and a first aid hut in the tea gardens.

Marjorie Kirkham has been in Helsby for 89 years and remembers her husband-to-be taking her courting on Helsby Hill. He claimed the lights were as good as Blackpool as they couldn't afford to go to the seaside resort itself! National occasions have been celebrated by bonfires on Helsby Hill many times, including Queen Victoria's jubilee and the accessions of King Edward VII and King George V. Bonfires are now forbidden.

It was possible to drive up to the summit via Harmer's Farm but now you have to walk the last part along a track. This track joined Hill Road North and Hill Road South and passed by Ben's Quarry and Harmers Wood. The lane was originally called Amoss Lake Lane and later Armers Lane which is where the name Harmers came from. A feature of this track, as it passes through the rock, are the chisel marks of the quarrymen which can be clearly seen. The track was passable by car until about the 1950s and we are told the route through the rock was much deeper than it is today.

Near the summit sits Harmer's Lake which was frequently visited by people for bathing and where they could hire paddle boats in the summer and skate on the ice when there was a severe winter. The lake was probably originally dug as a marl pit.

Helsby Scouts were formed in 1908 and have often

Harmer's Lake, January 1st 1914

Captured Memories across the Hillforts of Cheshire - Helsby

Helsby Scouts camping near Harmer's Lake

camped near to Harmer's Lake since the first camp there in about 1910.

Graham Hillyer of Harmer's Lake Farm took over the farm about 20 years ago. At that time the lake was black and full of rubbish which he cleared out about 12 years ago. When the lake was dredged he eventually came to a pure white 'sand/clay' mixture which would have been the pond lining and the base of the marl pit that was originally dug here. The pond is fed by a spring.

In doing the dredging, he found 100's of golf balls. He was approached by an American some years ago who purchased all the American antique golf balls for a substantial sum of money but he wasn't interested in the English ones which Mr Hillyer still has. These include examples of the balls produced by BICC including the Mersey, Imperial, National, Cestrian and later the Link. He didn't find any examples of clubs thrown into the lake in exasperation as the game was played by 'gentlemen' in those days! He also recovered a large number of bottles and jars.

WE NOW HAVE GOOD STOCKS OF

The B.I. STANDARD BALL

MADE TO COMPLY WITH THE NEW REGULATIONS OF THE RULES OF GOLF COMMITTEE, WHICH COME INTO FORCE ON 1st MAY 1921

This Ball is the equal of any other Ball on the Market, but the price is

only **2/6** each

THE B.I IS ALSO MADE IN 31 DWT AND FLOATING WEIGHT

BRITISH INSULATED AND HELSBY CABLES LTD.
HELSBY, near WARRINGTON

The local residents remember going into Harmer's Lake, not so much for the swimming but to collect the golf balls from the missed shots from the nearby golf course. They sold them back to the golfers at 6 old pence which was a lot of money in those days.

Further east is Harmer's Wood, previously known as the Rough Lot or the Pine Wood or the Old Quarry Wood before becoming Harmer's Wood sometime after World War 2.

Helsby Golf Ball

The wood was cut down in 1925, possibly during a very hard winter and was also burnt down during the Second World War by German bombers jettisoning bombs that had not been used over the docks in Liverpool. The present wood was purchased from the Cholmondeley Estate in June 2007 and is managed by the Friends of Harmers Wood Trust.

Firs Farm on Hill Road North used to be a tea and sweet shop. During the war a bomb went through the roof of the shed where the nanny goat lived and made a crater but didn't hurt the goat. Luckily none of the houses was damaged but the tea shop was destroyed.

Ben's Quarry, now within the wood, was planned in 1830 by Benjamin Morris after negotiations with the 4th Marquis of Cholmondeley and work stated in 1831 but closed by 1836. It was reopened in 1868 to provide stone for the 'new' Helsby church of St Paul's. Hillside Cottage on Hill Road North was built in 1854 and became a pub for the quarrymen. It was also known as Toothill or Teuthill Beer House. Teuthill is from the old-English 'teutian' which means a lookout place.

The Helsby Official Guide cover about 1950

Nowadays, the hillside is covered with trees and scrub but in the 1940s this was not the case. The hillside was covered in a mixture of gorse, heather and Vaccinium myrtillus; the bilberry or whinberry/whimberry as it is known in Cheshire. The hillside was grazed and, sad to say, fires were commonplace which kept the vegetation in check so the escarpment was much more dramatic and the 'face' on Helsby Hill was clearly seen. One older resident described the hillside as a 'like a pile of books pushed backwards – the different geological layers were clearly visible'.

At that time the whinberry was collected by the local children on the hill and made into pies but the locals invariably lost out after the Warrington Walking Week when the hillside was stripped of the fruit.

Another factor that probably contributed to the change in the vegetation was the spread of myxomatosis. This disease of rabbits decimated the rabbit population and allowed young saplings to survive and grow. In the 1950s the rabbit population of the UK was vast; perhaps 100 million animals. The South American myxoma virus was introduced into Australia in 1950 and infected rabbits were released in the Paris area by a scientist studying the virus. Subsequently the disease reached the UK in 1953 where it spread like wildfire. Nowadays the rabbit population has become largely immune to the disease and rabbit populations are once more on the increase. Incidentally, there are no records of rabbits in the UK prior to the twelfth century so our iron-age ancestors would not have recognised these animals. Rabbits were probably introduced by the Normans. Black rabbits are not uncommon and are known as clargymen or clergymen in Cheshire.

Helsby Hill - note the absence of tree cover

The hill once had a more gruesome past as it was the site of a gibbet. Many publications refer to a notorious robber named Lowndes who was hanged in 1798. He had stolen mail bags in 1795 and disappeared, only to be spotted in Exeter three years later and brought back to Chester for trial and execution on the hill. Research by Sue Lorimer suggests that the dates may be confused. There is reference to the execution of Lowndes in 1791. The trial was said to have cost £2000 and he was hanged in chains on Helsby Hill but the gibbet pole was cut down by some people in the neighbourhood and was not erected again. The history of the long life of crime of Lowndes can be found in a chronicle of Cheshire crimes 1612 – 1912.

High on Helsby Hill is an old water storage tower to supply the village but it is now covered by trees. It was fitted with a spherical bucket mounted on the top. This moved up when water was pumped from the Helsby Water Pumping Station at Three Ways Garage on Chester Road to show when the reservoir was full.

From the vantage point on the hill, the layout of Helsby can be seen. Helsby owes its development to two major influences. In 1850 the Birkenhead, Lancashire and Cheshire Junction Railway Company built their line and in 1863 the Helsby junction was created. As a result, together with a plentiful supply of water, the decision was taken to move the Telegraph Manufacturing Company from Neston

Captured Memories across the Hillforts of Cheshire - Helsby

and the Britannia Telegraph works was built. This developed into BICC and the growth of Helsby as we now know it. The company was started by George and James Taylor and originally occupied 1.5 acres but grew to cover an area of 80 acres and employed 3000 people. Unfortunately BICC closed down and the site is now largely occupied by Tesco's but the residential village remains.

Traffic congestion in Helsby was alleviated by the construction of the M56 which started in 1968 and was opened in January 1971. It can be clearly seen, and heard, from the summit. The coastline at one time would have roughly followed the line of the current M56.

Mrs Ivy Taylor, retired postlady, remembers the Helsby Hill Races. They would start from the BICC sports field, run up the hill and down again, on the annual sports day. The Old Post office, now converted to a house, used to be Clark's shop and they would cater for the Sunday School picnics on the hill, often for Liverpool children. They would 'deliver' the picnics to the hilltop.

John Deardon told us more about the hill races. "I've checked my race records, and can find only one time when I ran the Helsby Hill Race, on 2 October 1988. Of course it could have been held in other years round about that time, but if so I didn't run it. It was organised, so far as I remember, by Helsby Running Club. The race started on the Parish Field, crossed the main road, went up the gully (the one that goes over the bridge over Old Chester Road), turned left on Alvanley Road, going downhill for about 100 yards, then swung right on to the half-way path, carried on to the other end, then doubled back to take the path to the

A view of Helsby from the Hill

top of the hill, down the other side to Hill Road South, then right into Alvanley Road, back on to the half-way path for the second and third laps. On the third lap, instead of turning off Alvanley Road on to the half-way path, it carried on down Alvanley Road to the top of Crescent Drive, turned sharp left into Old Chester Road, as far as the junction with Robin Hood Lane, then right down Robin Hood Lane to the main road and into the Parish Field. There was also a Helsby Triple

Event. It comprised three legs - the hill leg (which I ran), a cycle leg then a road leg. I ran it three times (I think it was held only three times) on 12 July 1986, 11 July 1987 and 16 July 1988. It started somewhere on the Latham Avenue estate, turned right into Robin Hood Lane, went as far as the junction with Old Chester Road, then went up the gully, turned left at the top, into Alvanley Road, then on to the half-way path and followed the same route as the Helsby Hill Race as far as the descent of Hill Road South, then turned left on to Alvanley Road and carried on towards Manley as far as the dip before Symonds Hill (I think). There the runners handed over to the cycle leg (I don't know where that went), and the cyclists then handed over to the road runners (I don't know where they went, either, except that I remember that they came up Burrows Lane). I think the race was organised by Helsby Running Club." Jim Lloyd remembered that his father had won the Helsby Hill race in the 1950s.

Janet Ford has memories of the hill. She took part in the peregrine watch, in about 2004 and told us that her house faces the hill, and the nest was in full view under a crag. She joined a rota to watch through binoculars 24-hours a day until the birds fledged. One day she spotted a boy climbing along the hill below the top, out of sight of the RSPB man guarding above. He had a large sack and it was pretty obvious he was up to no good. She rang the contact she had, who then rang the RSPB man on top, who caught the lad!! The peregrines had 2 fledge that year. The following year it was decided to play it down, and keep a low profile in case of adverse publicity. The top of the hill was roped off, no mention made of nesting birds, and all was well. There are also peregrine nests on Beeston Castle crags (see page 94).

In 1975, when Janet and her husband moved to Helsby, St Paul's Church always had a Good Friday procession of witness, to carry a 12 foot wooden cross up to the hill. Folk took turns in teams of 4 to carry it. There were stops along the way for Bible readings, a hymn and prayer. She told us "We walked up Crescent Drive, then Alvanley Rd and onto the hill by Hill Rd South, with police stopping the traffic for us. Most of the congregations of both the Church and the Methodists took part. The cross stood for the Easter weekend and it was visible from the motorway. Sadly the cross has been vandalised over recent years, and the procession has only been along the A56 the length of Helsby."

Memories of Barbara Foxwell (nee Atherton)

"We came to live in Helsby when I was 2 years old. My father was working for Prescot Cables, and he chose to move to the countryside and work for the B.I.C.C. We were one of the very few families fortunate enough to own a car, a maroon Austin 10, and so we were able to go to see our grandparents often. We went over

Captured Memories across the Hillforts of Cheshire - Helsby

the terrifying Transporter Bridge in Runcorn, chained in an open cage as it creaked and swung across the Mersey and the Canal to Widnes. And the biggest landmark by far on our journey home was Helsby Hill, it stood out as a symbol of home for us. The 'Man's Face" on the crag was very clear and proud, because there was very little sign of trees or bracken to blur his features. My dad would always say "There HE is" as we came along the main road, almost as though the Hill were a living creature.

As children, we lived in Hillview Avenue, a cul-de sac, and we were free to use the whole area as our playground. Of course the little ones would play in the Avenue, games like hopscotch, marbles, skipping and chasing. Just 2 cars in the road, and they only came out to be cleaned. All around were fields for hide-and-seek and pits to fish in and trees to swing on.

And then as we grew older, about 9 or so, there was the Hill to climb. We would go in a gang up the Gully or through the Quarry, with a jam buttie and a drink, and stay all day. The older children would keep an eye on the younger ones. There were no marked or well worn paths, and we got lost, made dens, and even lit fires (my mum didn't know about that). We tried to make catapults and bows and arrows with twigs and string, but they never worked. We played tracking; running away and leaving little twig arrows or stones for the other team to follow. You could see sheer down to the Village, it was a clear high drop. Some boys would try to climb down the Slash Hooks on the front, but I was too scared. People did fall down and were hurt.

The Caves were further away, and very dark and damp. We screamed inside to make an echo, and once a tramp came scrambling out. We didn't know he was living there. We all ran like mad. The only rule was to be home before dark, and on the way home you could hear mothers calling their children in for tea.

But we were not the only people to use the Hill as a playground. There would be the excitement of meeting families from out of the village, as exotic-sounding to us as any foreigner now. We heard strange accents and dialects from Chester, Runcorn and Liverpool, which we could barely understand. Children are great talkers, and we made friends anyway. Or sometimes there would be fights between the bigger boys, but no-one really got hurt. You'd be too frightened to tell your mum. When I moved away briefly to live, the thing I missed most, apart from my family, was the sight of the Hill."

Memories of some of the members of Helsby Tuesday Club

The Club meets in the Helsby Community Centre each week. Many of the ladies made reference to the old Frodsham dialect and an example is shown below. Luckily, for the editors, we didn't need a translator during our visit!

FLUMMOX THA CHILLDA WI FRATSAM AND HELSBY TALK...
EVER heard of the Frodsham/Helsby Alphabet?
You may just understand some of the following:

A is fer axing fer summat thas not got.
B is fer borkin chillda do it a lot.
C is fer clawpin thee butter on bread.
D is fer dancers tha goss up ta bed.
E is fer essole tha sits rind at neet.
F is fer flummoxed tha can't get it reet.
G is fer gawless actin the foo.
H we neer used except when at skoo.
I is fer ikin like a kie wi its ern.
J is fer juft can fair gie thee a turn.
K is fer kebbly it rocks quate a bit.
L is fer Lozzack tha does nowt but sit.
M is fer mard it means soft as muck.
N is fer nonk tha gets fer givin owd buck.
O is fer occud not seef on thee feet.
P is fer puthree tha can fair feel th eet.
Q is fer quayat shurrup and be still.
R is fer rammy neer as a swill.
S is fer slotherin thee feet on th flewer.
T is fer torm thats wen tha faws ower.
U is fer unyun tha likes boilt in a pot.
V is fer varmint a mace or a rot.
W is fer weeges wen thy gets thee dosh.
X is fer hexlunt wen tha tries to talk posh.
Y is fer yoskin it can put thee ta bed.
Z is fer zonk means a clite rind thee yed.

A list of Cheshire dialect words can also be found at www.cheshirelittlefolk.co.uk and clicking on 'Old Cheshire Dialect'.

"I'm Chester born and bred, and our Holiday for the year was to come to Helsby Hill for a day trip. We came on the Crosville Bus or the train. When we got to Helsby we used to go to Jones's sweet shop on the main road first, for a bottle of Ginger Beer. It was a stone bottle, those things with 2 handles on the side. You'd pay for the bottle, and when you brought it back you got 6d. We would play hide and seek on the Hill. My mum used to make the arrangements and we took half the street with us, not just us. Then to finish we would walk to Clark's Field, for the swings and little roundabouts. That was our holiday."

(Margaret Ellis)

'There used to be little boats on Harmer's Lake, you could go for a sail if you had the money. We would swim in the lake as well. The Caves were open, you could go inside. Ginny Greenteeth lived in one."

'I remember Sunday School trips coming from Liverpool to picnic on Helsby Hill"

(Elizabeth Fowler)

"We would bring the children from our street in Liverpool for a day on the Hill. It was a big treat from the School."

"We carry The Easter Cross to the top of Helsby Hill on Good Friday. The tradition started in about 1976. Robin Howard was the Vicar of St. Paul's Church, and he started it. We carried The Cross from the Church car park, down to The Methodist Chapel, then up Crescent Drive, along Alvanley Road, and up Hill Road. It takes 2 people to carry it. Maybe we started in the Queen's Jubilee year. About 30 people join in the procession, from all churches."

"There was a Peregrine Watch on the Hill and the RSPB used the bunker for the storage of their equipment."

"There used to be The Hill Race and men came from all over to run up the Hill. It was organised by BICC and was going for about 50 years."

"We bought our cottage in 1947 and the hillside was totally different to today. The birches and holly weren't there and that was why the whinberries grew. My son used to play on the hill but only as high as the Carriage Way. He had an egg timer around his neck which was set to ping when it was time for him to come home for his lunch."

(Angela Green)

"There are several caves in the hillside with 2 large ones near Hill Road. These were locally known as the conker caves because of the Horse Chestnuts which grew there. They were also referred to as Billy's Helsby parlour and Jenny Greenteeth's but the origins are now obscure."

Jimmie Lloyd says that Jenny Greenteeth refers to a cave on the front of the hill which had two moss-covered boulders on each side – hence the green teeth. Sue Lorimer has researched the 'sandman' of Helsby who was probably William (Billy) Tweedle. Billy operated in about 1880 and extracted sand for delivery around the district for sanding floors. A small oval of land at the junction of Cobblers Lane and Hill Road North was designated in 1797 for common use to extract marl, gravel, clay etc. This is likely to be the 'sandy hole' where the caves were hollowed out to extract the sand.

Jenny (or Ginny) Greenteeth is a folklore character peculiar to Lancashire, Cheshire and Shropshire. She was thought to be a malignant spirit that lurked beneath the green weeds that covered stagnant pools of water or in tree tops, where she could be heard moaning at night. In some tales she took the form of a very thin old woman with green skin, green teeth, long green hair, long finger nails, a pointed chin and very big eyes. She appears to have been used as a 'bogey' to frighten children in to staying away from potentially dangerous places and was even used to scare children into cleaning their teeth properly.

According to the Countryfile Magazine, the true story of Jenny Greenteeth, or Jenny Greenfield as she was really known, starts in the village of Singleton in Lancashire. She was a prim woman whose main passion was for her garden. To help in this task she employed a handsome local man called Sam and became besotted with him. Unfortunately the love was not reciprocated and Sam married another. Jenny turned into a bitter and twisted woman. She neglected her garden and vandalised the village and the surrounding countryside. Her last mortal act was to attempt to poison the village well with weed-killer but instead she toppled in and was drowned in the icy waters. Ever since, she has lived on as a malevolent spirit haunting the countryside.

It is well worth visiting the Helsby Community Centre as there is an excellent display of photographs there. These are part of the collection put together by James (Jimmie) Lloyd. He was born in Helsby in 1943 but is a third generation Helsby resident. The photographs are part of collections from his parents and grandparents but to which he has added when he has come across items.

Helsby Golf Club

Helsby Golf Club was formed in 1901. However, the course itself began in 1902 when the club moved onto 30 acres of land off Primrose Lane & Towers Lane, near to today's 10th hole. In 1915, with the lease on the original Towers Lane land running out, the club moved to the top of Helsby hill, adjacent to Harmer's Lake and built a 9-hole course. The club remained until 1936 when plans for a new course on Towers Lane were prepared by the champion golfer and renowned course architect James Braid. This new course occupied the land which is now the front 9 holes. In 1964, additional land was purchased on the opposite side of Towers Lane. Plans were then drawn up for what is now the back 9 holes and Helsby Golf Club became a full 18-hole golf course in 1968.

The history of the 'back of the hill' course is highly relevant as the third green and 4th tee were within the Iron Age hillfort!

The following information was extracted from the Club minutes.
On the 12th September 1914, an Extraordinary General Meeting was called and agreed to obtain land on Helsby hill at a rental of £70 per annum on a ten year lease and a house which could be let at about £15 per year. In October 1914, it was agreed that Sunday play should be allowed provided that no servant of the club be called upon and that no caddies be employed. In March 1915, the first meeting in the pavilion on the new course was held. It was proposed that members of the club who had joined the forces be allowed to retain their membership during the war without subscription and the club wish them the very best of luck and a safe return. No shooting be allowed on the course as it was considered unsafe for members but this was rescinded in 1928 when it was resolved that any member may shoot rabbits over the course and that the groundsmen share them.

In August 1915, Mr Cooper - the tenant of the house on the new course - was offered the work of looking after the links two days a week at the price of 5 shillings per day (about 25p) including the mowing and rolling of the greens when necessary twice a week. In Nov 1916, an offer to rent the course for sheep grazing was accepted at 25 Shillings per month, to graze about 50 sheep. By March 1920, the first matches were agreed to take place with Runcorn Golf Club. It is of interest to note that in 1922, it was agreed that the groundsmen be allowed to grow potatoes between the third green and the fourth tee which are believed to be within the hillfort.

At the AGM in 1923, Mrs J Edmonson was elected Captain of Helsby Golf Club and was requested to continue with making teas!

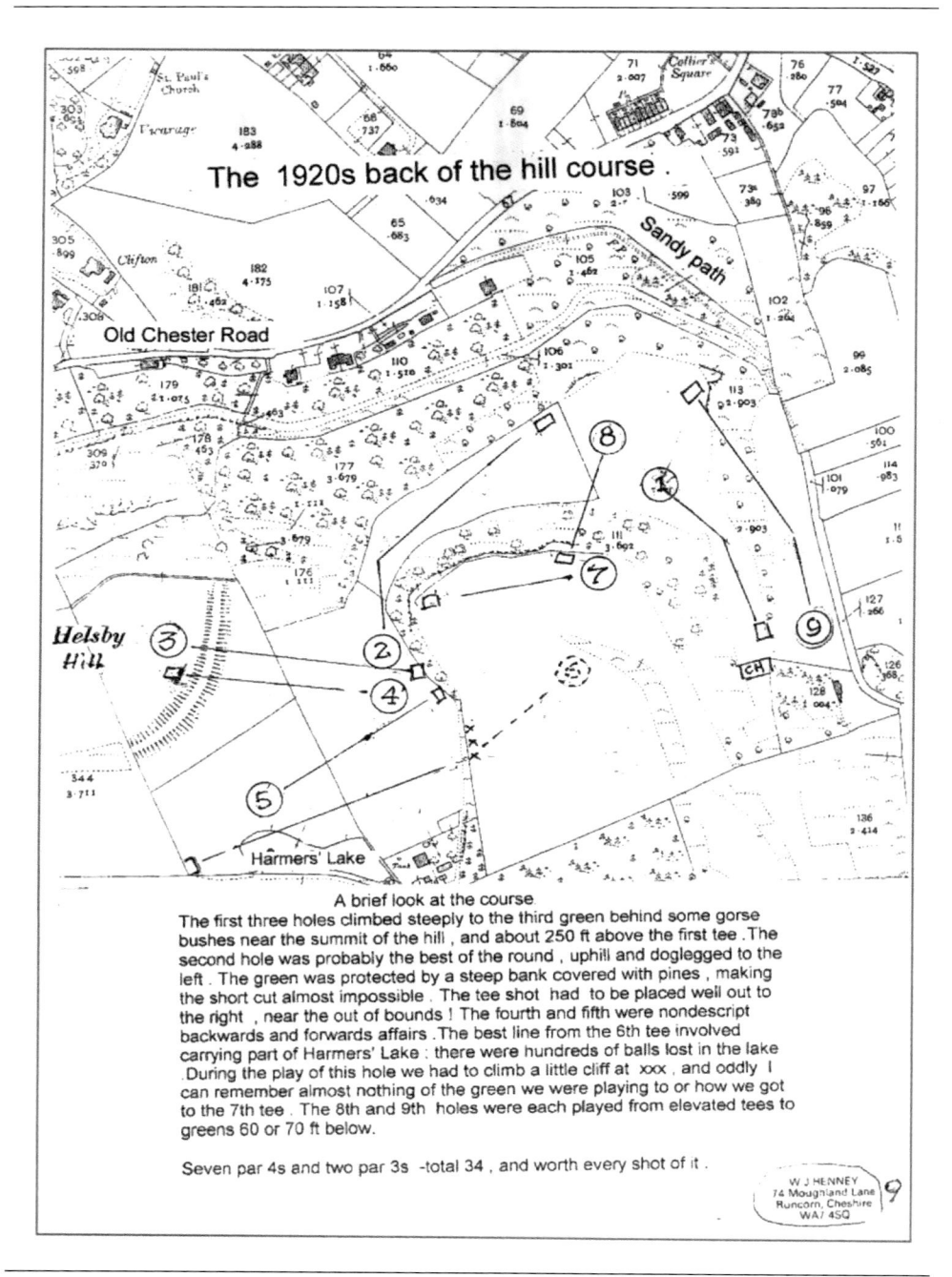

Captured Memories across the Hillforts of Cheshire - Helsby

The 1920s back of the hill course

A brief look at the course

The first three holes climbed steeply to the third green behind some gorse bushes near the summit of the hill, and about 250 ft above the first tee. The second hole was probably the best of the round, uphill and doglegged to the left. The green was protected by a steep bank covered with pines, making the short cut almost impossible. The tee shot had to be placed well out to the right, near the out of bounds! The fourth and fifth were nondescript backwards and forwards affairs. The best line from the 6th tee involved carrying part of Harmers' Lake : there were hundreds of balls lost in the lake. During the play of this hole we had to climb a little cliff at xxx , and oddly I can remember almost nothing of the green we were playing to or how we got to the 7th tee. The 8th and 9th holes were each played from elevated tees to greens 60 or 70 ft below.

Seven par 4s and two par 3s -total 34, and worth every shot of it.

W J HENNEY
74 Moughland Lane
Runcorn, Cheshire
WA7 4SQ

14

In 1931, the groundsmen's wages for a 48 hour week were agreed at £135 per year (2 pounds 12 shillings per week). In the winter the groundsmen only worked 40 hours per week but the accumulated difference between 40 and 48 hrs had to be worked off in the growing season at the discretion of the greens committee.

It wasn't until 1933 that Mersey Power's offer to install electricity to the pavilion was accepted.

The lease of the golf course on Helsby Hill was due to expire on 1st February 1937. The original agreement leased the land from Mr Arrowsmith who had since died, and his estate had passed to Mr Lewis Brandeth & Miss Brandeth.

From April 1936, discussions took place with Mr Brandeth regarding the renewal of the lease. It was fairly obvious from the initial meetings that both parties to the agreement were in some sort of dispute. It was alleged by the landlord that the farmhouse which was the clubs responsibility was in a deplorable state. This, the committee strongly denied stating that the house was in very good order apart from some work required to the outside. Other arguments concerned the rent and on land which the landlord, but not the club, wished to include. On 17th September 1936, it was announced that 2 members of the committee had obtained an option from Mr T Noden on 50 acres of pasture land with an entrance on to the main road near Horne Mill at £2 per acre. The committee decided the terms of the renewed lease of the hillside course were not acceptable and to terminate the tenancy as from 1st February 1937. It was estimated that a sum of £513 was required for a scheme to transfer the course to the new site and this sum was borrowed from the members.

The Club House at Helsby Golf Club

The task of transferring to the new course involved moving the clubhouse, mowers, rollers and all other machinery. Fences had to be repaired and some broken windows in the stable had to be made good. Disputes continued and led to a court case between the club and Mr Brandeth.

Climbing at Helsby and Frodsham

The rocks at Helsby have long been the playground of Merseyside climbers.

When John Laycock published "Some Gritstone Climbs" in 1913 he recorded some twenty-five climbs at Helsby in his book. At that stage just seven routes merited the "severe" rating, among them the Overhanging Crack which was reckoned to be one of the hardest 'gritstone' climbs in England.

The mid-twenties saw considerable activity with members of the Climbers' Club, among them C.W. Marshall, producing a number of difficult and classic climbs. During the period 1928-29 the Wayfarers' Club put up twenty-three climbs, four of them led by F.E. Hicks and with the magnificent Colin Kirkus pioneering the other nineteen, including the still sensational Flake Crack. This climb has undoubtedly claimed more lives than any other single route at Helsby, most notably that of C.W. Marshall himself who died of injuries sustained attempting the first solo early in 1928.

Climbing on Helsby's gritstone crags

Menlove Edwards, one of the most important figures in British climbing, honed his legendary strength at Helsby where he achieved the first lead of Flake Crack three years after Marshall's death. Other great pioneers included Colin Kirkus and A.B.Hargreaves. John Menlove Edwards (18 June 1910 – 2 February 1958) was one of the leading British rock climbers of the interwar period and wrote poetry based on his climbing experiences. He was born near Southport and studied medicine at Liverpool University, where he became a child psychiatrist. During World War II he was a conscientious objector. He had an unhappy personal life, partly as a result of being a homosexual at a time when this was illegal. This unhappiness made him vulnerable to bouts of depression and he committed suicide with a cyanide capsule in 1958. His first ascents include many of the now-classic rock routes on the crags of the Llanberis Pass in Snowdonia such as "Flying Buttress", "Spiral Stairs", "Crackstone Rib", "Nea" and "Brant".

Captured Memories across the Hillforts of Cheshire - Helsby

Colin Kirkus, one of the best known British rock climbers between the two world wars, 'bouldered' at Helsby in the 1930s. The red sandstone bluff above the village of Helsby offers climbs of from 20 to 50 feet, requiring gymnastic ability and strong fingers. Its friable nature prompted the use of a top rope by climbers in Kirkus's generation - at least on first tries. The standards at Helsby were exceptionally high, compared to other climbing areas in the British Isles. You can read about Kirkus in "Hands of a Climber: A Life of Colin Kirkus" by Steve Dean (1993). Kirkus wrote one of the finest instruction books ever written "Let's go Climbing!". Kirkus was lost in a bombing raid over Germany during the Second World War.

When the Wayfarers' Club published its small pocket guide in 1946, energetically assisted by the Liverpool University Mountaineering Club which cycled to Helsby on frequent Sundays, only obvious lines of ascent had been described. Climbers had no hardware at their disposal, only a hemp rope and sometimes a sling or two for the protection of followers, not the leader! New generations of climbers have addressed themselves to numerous harder problems despite the encroaching vegetation. Almost every foot of Helsby now seems to have been explored.

Colin Kirkus

It was during the early fifties that Hugh Banner started to visit the Helsby crags and another significant achievement around this time was the ascent of Quarry Buttress by John Evans.

Hugh Irving Banner, rock climber and engineer was born in Crosby, Lancashire on 31 Aug 1933 and died Bangor, Gwynedd 23 April 2007. He was one of the pioneers of the strenuous, fingery climbing on the forbiddingly steep limestone of Avon Gorge. He kept his standard topped up on the highly technical sandstone of his local crag at Helsby while based at his parental home in Lancashire. Banner soon became almost as famous for his feats of derring-do on his Vincent motorbike as on his climbs, reaching over 100mph on a straight bit of road going past Helsby Grammar School on the way to his local pub in Frodsham. In 1957 Banner revised Carsten's 1946 guide and the 5c grade appeared for the first time. The end of the decade saw the emergence, under the leadership of Banner, of the Helsby group which included a number of gifted climbers such as Ken Prandy and Jim O'Neill.

17

The Frodsham Buttresses were discovered around this time by the Helsby group. Jim O'Neill was especially active but a quick look at the names of the routes indicates that some of the best climbers of the day also passed this way, as evidenced by Crew's Arete, Banner's Route and Boysen's Route.

So thorough had been the Helsby group of the late fifties, activity slackened until the early eighties. Noted climbers of this time include Phil Davidson, Mike Collins, Tom Jones and Joe Healey. More recently Mike Collins, Pete Chadwick and Alan Cameron-Duff added some hard top rope problems to Helsby. Recent hard climbing has concentrated on the Frodsham crags by Ewan McCallum, Will Simm and Mike Collins.

Trig Point

On the top of Helsby Hill stands a concrete pillar which is known as a trig (or more correctly a triangulation) point (TP3723) and was erected by the Ordnance Survey. Few people take much notice of this structure but it played a major role in the mapping of the UK. The trig point used to be white but has now been painted green to try to prevent it being covered in graffiti.

The process of placing trig points on top of prominent hills and mountains began in 1935 to assist in the accurate retriangulation of Great Britain. In low lying or flat areas some trig points may be only a few metres above sea-level. When all the trig points were in place, it was possible, in clear weather, to see at least two other trig points from any one trig point. Careful measurements of the angles between the lines-of-sight of the other trig points then allowed the construction of a system of triangles which could then be referenced back to a single baseline to construct a highly accurate measurement system that covered the entire country.

This system improved upon the original mapping work that began in the 18th Century as cartographers rushed to survey and map the south coast in case of an invasion by Napoleon. These military objectives originated in the National Survey of the Board of Ordnance which was a fore-runner of the Ministry of Defence.

In most of the United Kingdom, trig points are truncated square concrete (occasionally stone) pyramids or obelisks tapering towards the top. On the top a brass plate with three arms and a central depression is fixed. A benchmark is set on the side, marked with the letters "OSBM" (Ordnance Survey Bench Mark) and the reference number of the trig point. Within the trig point, there are concealed mountings for a specialised theodolite, which was temporarily mounted on the trig point while measurements were taken.

The standard trig point design is credited to Brigadier Martin Hotine CMG CBE (1898–1968), the then head of the Trigonometrical and Levelling Division of the Ordnance Survey. Many of them are now disappearing from the countryside as their function has largely been superseded by aerial photography and digital mapping using lasers and GPS measurements.

Wartime observation post

The summit of Helsby hill was the site of a wartime observation post and later a cold war bunker.

The Helsby Post of the Royal Observer Corps has been described by Dennis Bates who lived at the Frodsham branch of the National Children's Home between 1934 and 1943. He also served in the Royal Observer Corps at the original 19 Group at Beckenham, Kent.

'Back in 1934 the Government announced that the air strength of the Royal Air Force would be increased. At the same time air-defence planning concerned itself with the new threat of the long-range bomber. The Defence Committee made a particularly important conclusion: 'That a highly organised intelligence system is essential for the rapid collection and distribution of information regarding the movements of friendly and hostile aircraft throughout the whole area of possible operation.' To implement this, the committee recommended that the existing Observer Corps of special constables that existed in the Southeast should be expanded to cover England roughly south of a line from Middlesbrough to Preston. Groups with operational areas would be formed and that for Manchester, designated Number 7 Group would be in Stage 3 effective from 1 March 1937 with full operational capability by 1 March 1939 because even at that time the Services were convinced war would come by that year. They were proved absolutely right.

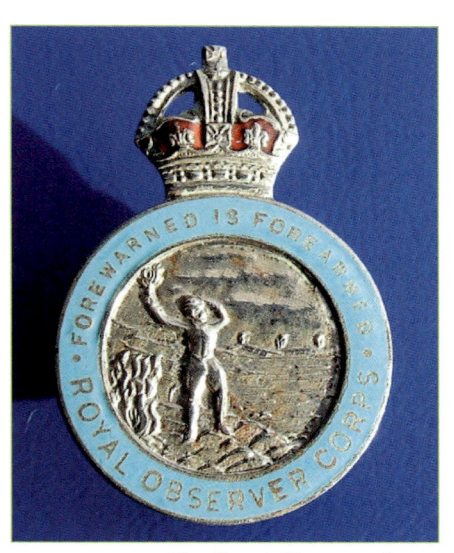

The Royal Observer Corps

No 7 Group's area was from Prestatyn, along the south bank of the Dee across mid-Cheshire around Manchester and up to embrace Preston and Blackpool. Its HQ or Centre was in the GPO building in Spring Gardens, Manchester until 1942 when it moved to Slade Lane, Levenshulme.

The surveying team were looking for sites for the network of posts that would cover the area. Posts would be on high or exposed ground, close to towns or villages and situated so that their theoretical operating area would have a radius of 5 miles touching on the operating area of the surrounding posts.

Post Fox 3 Helsby, OS Grid Reference J493764, opened in 1937. Middlewich was the location for Fox 1 and Fox 2 was at Tarporley. Each post had a head observer, usually in the rank of Chief Observer and an establishment of 20-24 male observers — women observers would come much later. All would be volunteers, live locally and not be paid except for a subsistence allowance. The job was to plot all aircraft movements in the vicinity by visual means in daytime and by "sound" plots at night. Operational duty was two men usually in 4-hour shifts, requiring twelve men for just a day and a night.

The post sited on Helsby Crag probably conformed to the customary shape of a sandbagged, dished circle within which was a plotting table marked with grid references of which the post was the centre point. The outline of the post can probably still be seen by the circular depression to the left of the trig point when looking north. A mechanical device that was mounted on the table could be moved round enabling an aircraft to be seen through the sighting mechanism and by estimating height and distance its actual grid position could be ascertained. One observer scanned the skies continuously often lying on their backs and using binoculars. The other wore a head and breast set, sighted the post instrument and gave the plot to Centre.

On the open landline connecting the posts in each cluster their colleagues could overhear the plot and make corrections to height, and four pairs of eyes were better than two. If this sounds primitive it was, but radar could not operate overland nor could it recognise the type of aircraft or distinguish between friend or foe. In fact the Observers became so proficient that they were as fast, or faster, than radar, the plots were accurate and relayed by GPO landline direct to the Observer Corps Centre, plotted on their table, but only hostile tracks were immediately told forward to Fighter Command. Thus the fighters could be vectored onto the enemy without the RAF's main plotting table being swamped with training aircraft, delivery flights, transport and all the other non-operational air movements.

It was a long hike uphill to Helsby post where the crew would have been frozen in the dead of winter, lashed by wind and soaked by rain; whatever the weather the plotting went on. Helsby Crag was particularly exposed and during the raids on Liverpool its crew had the added danger from stray bombs and shrapnel spraying from shell bursts.

These volunteers - later some were paid full time - did their normal daytime job and then a turn of duty. That duty for the entire Corps was to last for every minute for two thousand and eighty nine days from 24 August 1939 to 12 May 1945, four days after VE Day.

The strange thing was that it came to the notice of the powers that be that the key to fighting the Battle of Britain was the plotting of enemy raids by the Observer Corps without which Fighter Command was blind. Yet it was a bit infra dig that these chaps were dressed in their normal civilian gear, their only authority an Observer Corps brassard, were civilians and unpaid! You can imagine it - civvies playing a major role in a battle! So along came a uniform of sorts that gradually evolved into battle dress, head gear, forage cap or beret, a heavy duty Macintosh oilskin-lined. But their civilian status did remain, they were not subject to military discipline, yet they wore the Kings uniform and were part of Fighter Command. Without them the Battle of Britain could not have been fought and won, and in June 1941 the Corps was honoured with the granting by HM The King of the Royal Warrant,

Helsby post carried on in the re-birth of the Corps in 1947 becoming Jig 2 of 19 Group at the re-organisation of 1953 changing again in 1961 to Kilo 3 in 16 Group. When aircraft plotting gave way to nuclear burst/fall-out reporting in November 1959 Kilo 3 went underground in October 1968 still at the same location, with a new call sign of Bravo 3.

The Royal Observer Corps finally stood down as a field force on 30 September 1991. Possibly, just possibly, Kilo 3 remains securely battened down out of sight and out of mind on Helsby Crag." *(Editors' note – yes it does exist but is not securely battened down – see below)*

Mostly the Corps and its activities have remained shrouded in mystery. Just after the war The Aeroplane magazine summed up its achievements thus: 'The general public knew nothing of the activities of the ROC and little realised that the one organisation which was in closest contact with operations of war was this pseudo-military body. In fact the ROC was probably responsible for more damage to the enemy's war effort than most of our home-based military forces of a similar character, which must be unique in the annals of civilian national service'.

When they were building the Observer Corps post, a Frodsham chap called Bill Warburton who was working on the excavation found a little gold coin. It turned out to be Roman and was valued at £2,000.

There was an anti-aircraft gun site at Alvanley and a searchlight unit at the top of Primrose Lane. A bomb was dropped down here in Freshmeadow Lane. It didn't go off and the bottom six houses were evacuated, but it turned out to be a dud. What damage was done to these houses was caused by shrapnel from the anti-aircraft guns.

About 100 yards behind the Observation Post was a small hut erected by the Helsby Home Guard which was frequently manned by Geoffrey Monks. He wrote: "By the time of the nightly devastating air raids on Merseyside, our role had changed. The possibility of invasion had receded. Now, we were concerned with watching out for single or small parties of parachutists who were expected to slip in during the confusion of air raids. This meant a constant watch on the marshes at such times, Also, by then we had acquired a small hut on the hill about 100 yds. back from the Observer Corps Post. Evan Williams, who lived in Alvanley Drive, and myself were deemed to live the nearest to it, so when the warning sounded we made our way up there, past the water tower, where "The Spinney" now is.

I don't think members of the Royal Observer Corps (several of whom were ex Members of the Royal Flying Corps) were very impressed at being guarded by a seventeen year old with a rifle as big as him. However, nothing was ever said and they were quite friendly. Perhaps they were glad to see anybody up there in those circumstances. Once the AA guns opened up, the nearest lot was the 3.7 Battery in Alvanley, just at the back of us (Ted Heath's lot) the shrapnel would start bouncing off the rock. We certainly had a grandstand view of those raids, but like the people of Liverpool, were very glad when they became less frequent.

It was around the end of 1941 that Tony and I joined the regular forces, so, apart from snatches of information in my father's letters, I'm not sure what went on after that. I believe several new Members joined to replace those like ourselves who had left and the platoon went from strength to strength until disbanded."

Cold War Bunker

Now largely overgrown and vandalised, there are the remains of a cold war bunker on the top of Helsby Hill. Please note that the bunker is on private land.

Graham Hillyer, on whose land the bunker stands, remembers that the bunker was intact about 15 years ago with the original bunks and radio still in place. He lent the special key to the bunker to the RSPB at the time of the peregrine watch but unfortunately they lost it. The padlocks they then used to secure the bunker were not substantial enough and it was easily broken into and vandalised.

Captured Memories across the Hillforts of Cheshire - Helsby

The remains of the Cold War Bunker

The bunker was an extension of the work of the Royal Observer Corps which operated between 1925 and 1965. Their role was to track and monitor aircraft movements over the UK but the need for this diminished and ceased in 1965. However a new threat had emerged and in 1955 there was a perceived need to monitor nuclear blasts. The UK Warning and Monitoring Organisation (UKWMO) was born and 1,563 ROC underground bunkers were constructed about 7 - 8 miles apart around the UK.

The current condition of the bunker on Helsby Hill and a mock-up of what it could have looked like has been posted on 'YouTube' by Lee Oulton and can be viewed at http://www.youtube.com/watch?v=MC29SchAgtQ

Paul Heath has memories of the bunker.

"The Helsby Hill bunker was probably built in the 1950s in the early days of the Cold War and manned by mainly civilian volunteers. Originally set up to give early warning of air attack their main role after the war was radiation monitoring. They were later amalgamated into the UK Warning and Monitoring Organisation. They had a much bigger bunker near Wrexham and I remember that even in the mid-eighties they used to run exercises tracking the spread of radiation from theoretical Soviet attacks. They used to like to track the fallout from really big 100 megaton devices because these created the most interesting problems and I remember upsetting them by pointing out the biggest devices the Soviets then used were 5 megaton and these were targeted on the US missile bases - we would get 200 kiloton devices from SS20 missiles. All a bit academic as any of these monstrosities would ruin your day but it was typical of their well-intentioned amateurism. The ROC usually operated in teams of 3 manning a small bunker - usually just a single room built to a standard design. There were hundreds of these across the country including the one on Helsby Hill."

George and Mabel Coulter moved to Helsby in 1953 and George was a volunteer for the ROC between 1965 and 1981. George remembers:

"There were over 12 volunteers including my son, Hugh, for a year before he went to university, the O'Brien girls, Mr Salisbury, Eric Clover, and Peter Smith who was the chief observer. Mr Salisbury resigned when the girls were introduced to the squad. We had exercises at weekends tracking simulated radioactive clouds from different parts of the country. Our results had to be delivered very speedily to the headquarters in Shrewsbury. What was supposed to happen then or what we had to do if there had been a real cloud was unclear. We had clockwork instruments as there was no power to the bunker. It had two bunk beds but I can't remember them being used. The bunker had a hand pump to clear water that leaked through the lid and a chemical toilet but no water supply. The floor was concrete so it could be very cold. By the time I joined in 1965 our perception of a threat from a nuclear attack had largely diminished but I enjoyed the group and we had planning meetings in various Helsby pubs like the Horse and Jockey, The Robin Hood and The Railway."

In comparison, it should be noted that there was also another, larger bunker, in the neighbourhood. The Cheshire County Council site was "The Beacons" on Frodsham/Overton Hill.

Paul Heath has reported: "This was much bigger. I believe it was built in the early 1950s by the Royal Artillery as an Anti-Aircraft Control Centre for the North West Air Defence Region. It would have operated in much the same way as the control centres you see in films like The Battle of Britain. It had a large central well which I assume had a map table on which attacks could be plotted along with any fighter interceptors sent up to meet them. Of course they had radar but this was fairly crude and the info would have to be converted into a visual representation on a map. They were beginning to use surface-to-air missiles at this time but in the 50s would still rely heavily on anti-aircraft guns - though by this time they had crude computers which would use the info from radar about height and speed to target the guns. When I first went there were still a few bits of equipment scattered about but it was all fairly basic. The site was well-placed to cover the Liverpool docks which had particular significance in the event of a Soviet invasion of Western Europe. Liverpool was designated as the port of entry for US reinforcements, particularly their heavy equipment. An entire Armoured Corps with hundreds of tanks and other vehicles would cross the Atlantic by sea, land at Liverpool and be transported across the UK by rail. The County's Emergency Planning Team took over the site in the mid-eighties from the County Archivist. It had been used for storage but was most unsuitable and I think the change coincided with the development of the Duke Street Record Office. The site was then designated as the County's main emergency centre with the standby at County Hall. Of course not to be outdone the Districts had their own with varying degrees of sophistication. The Plan was that in the event of a nuclear war the Cheshire County Council Chief Executive would lock himself away in the Beacons with his Team and direct operations from there but the plan had numerous flaws. The "4 minute warning" didn't leave much time to go there, there was no provision for families and the communications facilities (not to mention sanitation) were woefully inadequate. Fortunately Emergency Planning thinking has moved on. So, all in all, the Beacons was something of a white elephant."

Martin Smith, previously of Cheshire County Council told us: "The last I heard was that the Fire Service wished to buy the Beacons as a centre for training fire-fighters in such things as using breathing apparatus - it would be perfect. I'm not sure what happened since."

Until recently the Beacon was featured on the Subterranean Britannica site (www.subbrit.org.uk) - they had a page on the Beacons, including photographs but it is no longer on the site but there may be ways of accessing older material.

References

1. 'Helsby Village' produced by Helsby Hillside Women's Institute 2007.
2. Frodsham and District Local History Journal, Issue 26, p3-4, 1998.
3. Helsby's Walk through History booklet.
4. Lowndes: 'Outrages, Fatal and Other. A chronicle of Cheshire Crime, 1612-1912' Derek Yarwood, 1991, Didsbury Press, Manchester. ISBN 1 872325 01 7.
5. www.helsbygolfclub.org and go to 'Our Club' and 'History of the Club'.
6. "Hands of a Climber: A Life of Colin Kirkus" by Steve Dean (1993).
7. Sandstone Climbing in Cheshire and Merseyside by Alan Cameron-Duff and Peter Chadwick. 1998 Published by Stone Publishing and Design, Waterfoot, Rossendale, Lancashire BB4 9AG
8. Observation post: Frodsham Local History Journal Issue 36 page 25
9. Observation Post: Frodsham Local History Journal Issue 18 page 13
10. Observation post: Frodsham Local History Journal Issue 17 page 13
11. Bunker on Helsby Hill http://www.youtube.com/watch?v=MC29SchAgtQ
12. The Beacon was featured on the Subterranean Britannica site (www.subbrit.org.uk)
13. Jenny Greenteeth. Countryfile Magazine, Spring 2011, p 114.

Captured Memories across the Hillforts of Cheshire

Artist's impression of Woodhouse Hillfort by Dai Owen

Cleared ramparts, 2010

LIDAR view of Woodhouse – see page xi

WOODHOUSE HILLFORT

27

Woodhouse Hillfort

Woodhouse fort attracts far less attention and people walking the Sandstone Trail frequently do not realise they are passing an Iron Age site. However the hamlet of Woodhouses is of the same significance as Helsby on maps from the late 18th century. The hamlet lies below the escarpment under the hillfort.

Excavations of the hillfort were made in 2009.

19th century pipe bowl from the rampart rubble

Find from the dig

Cross section across the rampart at Woodhouse, 2009

The Hamlet of Woodhouses

Pauline Scott told us about the cruck barn which once stood at Woodhouse Farm, Tarvin Road, Frodsham and is now located at Tatton Park Knutsford. Her father (who believed that the barn was of significant historical interest) had been trying to raise interest in the building for several years to see if it could be protected and preserved as the local council were saying it was an eyesore and should be demolished. By chance he met the County Archaeologist at a function and the rest is history, as they say!

The Barn at Woodhouse Farm circa 1975

Here is the link to the Tatton Park site which has some more information: http://www.tattonpark.org.uk/Attractions/Old+Hall/cruckbarn.htm. Briefly, the story is as follows:

The Cruck Barn at Tatton Old Hall started life at the beginning of the 17th century and is a fine example of a style once common in the Midlands and North, and is constructed from a series of paired timbers called crucks, each of which forms a shape like the letter A.

Dilapidated and crumbling and expensive to restore, the barn was roofed with rusting corrugated iron. Several of its crucks had slipped off their plinths making total collapse imminent. Since old maps showed that a barn had once existed at the Old Hall, Tatton, the opportunity was taken to accept this generous offer of a valuable example of Cheshire's vernacular architecture.

Undeterred by its condition, a team of one joiner and a small number of unskilled young people working under a job creation scheme carefully dismantled the barn. Much of the timber recovered was re-used and, working from a prepared set of

Lancashire & Cheshire
ANTIQUARIAN SOCIETY

24 Edale Grove,
Sale,
Cheshire, M33 4 RG.

24th March 1975.

Re: Barn, Travin Road, Woodhouses, Frodsham.
       Map Reference, SJ 507763.

Of cruck construction, originally built as a 4 bay corn barn with a threshing bay and 3 storage bays. It has its long axis approximately east/west.

The north side of the barn is the better preserved, the timber framing being almost intact (brick infill now replaces the original wattle and daub) and this side of the roof has much of an early covering of ling which grows on the hillside to the east.

The date would seem to be fairly late for a cruck building – about 1600.

Truss 1 (the east end of the barn) is missing and has been replaced by brick.

Truss 2 has failed at the apex and a kingpost has been added (re-used cruck timber showing half-lapped joints) in order to stabilise. This truss also shows other re-used timber.

Between trusses 2 and 3 is the threshing bay.

The base of the south blade of truss 3 has sunk, causing the whole truss to tilt with a resulting displacement of the ridge purlin.

Truss 5 (the west end of the original barn) shows the two blades truncated and enveloped in brick.

The main timbers show little sign of deterioration; the barn as a whole is a good example of cruck construction and would be an ideal subject either for restoration or for re-erection on an open-air museum or similar site.

D.G. Richbell.

Captured Memories across the Hillforts of Cheshire - Woodhouse

drawings, it was reconstructed and restored on its current site. Its rebuilding provided many skills for young people.

The barn's four sets of crucks are equally spaced along its 70 feet length and together with its timber-framed walls stand on a sandstone plinth. The plinth continues across doorways to form a 'thresh hold', literally to hold threshed corn within the building. Originally the in-fills of the frames would have been wattle and daub but at some point were replaced with brickwork, as bricks became cheaper and more readily available. This material would have made the building more weather and animal proof and easier to maintain. The roof is thatched with reeds whose butt ends jut out and form the eaves drop, which casts rainwater away from the building.

The barn at Woodhouses and restored at Old Hall, Tatton Park

Pauline Scott also told us of the communal dipping well at Woodhouses which she has never known to dry up.

The dipping well

Around the Hillfort

"We used to ride our ponies up to Woodhouse Hill. There was a good view from the top, no Silver Birches just some seedlings. We used the outer wall of the Fort as a jumping ground for the ponies. There were no pathways; we all wandered around. It was too steep to climb with the pony so we came along Bottom Lane. We made a track to ride down. That was fast."

(Sheila Aukland)

> **Woodhouse**
>
> Flaming ramparts exude the sun
> Saluting a laden hunter,
> Whose home-fire pants out tangy smoke
> Reviving his uncertain hope
>
> That all things are as they should be
> Within the fermenting fold. There
> Young revellers dance as night dawns
> And the soothsayer sings a song
>
> Of a far changed distant time,
> When earth, flowers and trees return,
> So shrouding their tenable scarp
> As the wealthy river departs.
>
> *Barry Smith, Manley Common,*
> *February 2011*

Near to the fort lie Dunsdale Hollow, Abraham's Leap and Jacob's Ladder. The latter was a rough flight of steps cut into the soft sandstone and was in use until the 1990s but wear and tear meant that they were replaced by wooden steps, known as Bakers Dozen in memory of Jack Baker who was instrumental in the development of the Sandstone Trail. Abraham's Leap steps were cut around 1900 when the coming of the railway to Frodsham opened up the countryside to a whole new generation of visitors.

The Sandstone Trail was one of the first such routes in the country pioneered by

Cheshire County Council's Countryside Recreation Department. The original trail was opened in 1974 and was only 16 miles long from Delamere to Duckington but it was soon extended up to Beacon Hill near Frodsham and Grindley Brook to the south. In the late 1990s links were extended to Frodsham and Whitchurch to make it more accessible to public transport.

Alongside the Frodsham to Dunsdale section there is much evidence of the quarrying activities and the walls are covered with the graffiti of long-gone visitors as well as present day ones. Our fore-fathers took a great deal more trouble with their name carving than the crude scratches of more recent times. Some of the graffiti shows a high degree of carving skill and date back to the 1840s. A way to amuse your children, or you, is to search for the earliest date, as well as carved faces, regimental insignia and relative's initials. This does have a more serious purpose as the graffiti was obviously carved after the quarrying so can give an indication of the date the quarry activity ceased.

Dunsdale Hollow

Dunsdale derives from the unromantic name for 'dung valley' but is far more scenic these days. Dunsdale Hollow is situated on the western edge of Frodsham and is near to the Mesolithic and Iron Age sites. The area was extensively quarried primarily for work associated with the Manchester Ship Canal and possibly the Liverpool Docks. In about 1872, it was accessible by a road that is now the Frodsham Carriage Drive. The upper reaches were about 20 feet wide but have now degenerated and it was thought it originally went all the way to Woodhouse Hill and Dunsdale House built in 1856. Dunsdale House was an outpost of the National Children's Home during World War 2. In the grounds there is a strange stone built chamber which has been variously described as a cock-fighting pit, a hermit's shelter (having your own live-in hermit was very fashionable at one time) or an ice house – take your pick! Another imposing house along the carriageway is Erindale which was built for the Crossfield family linked to the Unilever Company. At one time this was used as Netherton House School which shut in the late 1960s.

Dunsdale Hollow has a long history of use as a practice firing range and musket balls have been found as well as bullets from the Lee-Enfield rifle used in World War 1. During the Second World War it was again used for firing practice including American soldiers who were stationed in Warrington and at a camp in Delamere. These soldiers brought the newly developed, exotic tins of Nescafe coffee, first produced in 1937, which they gave to local residents as their first taste of the now commonplace drink.

Captured Memories across the Hillforts of Cheshire - Woodhouse

Stray finds of gun cartridges and mortar shrapnel found during excavations

Local Home Guard groups including the 13th Cheshire Brigade Home Guard and the Frodsham Home Guard used Dunsdale Hollow for firing and bomb throwing practice.

Frodsham and district was alive with military activity during World War 2 and thousands of troops must have been stationed in the area. Battalions included the South Lancs, the Cheshires, the Royal Welch Fusiliers, the Middlesex Regiment, a section of the RAMC, a unit of the Royal Artillery, the ATS and Women's Land army.

In the summer of 1987 Dunsdale Hollow was declared as a site of special scientific interest (SSSI) because of its unusual flora.

Frodsham Golf Club

Adjacent to Dunsdale Hollow lays Frodsham Golf Club. The first Frodsham Golf Club, which dated back to the late 1870s, ceased to exist in 1924. This old, nine hole course on land known locally as Cave Fields is just across the road from the current Club. The steep inclines and deep valleys must have provided a tough challenge for the golfers of yesteryear. The "new" Frodsham Golf Club which opened in July 1990 is said to be equally as demanding as the old course but over far less difficult terrain.

Over the years it has hosted several major professional and amateur events. Frodsham offers a unique blend of old and new amid 130 acres of rolling Cheshire countryside. After a hard game of golf you can enjoy a drink in the Club House, while the restaurant and Spikes Bar are open for lunch and evening meals.

Up to the late 1980s the site of the present Frodsham Golf Club was a dairy and arable unit known as Upper Mickledale Farm which dates from around 1785. The farmland comprised of 106 acres of free draining sandy and medium loam soils. The natural draining and pleasantly undulating topography of the land lent itself perfectly to the development of the golf course that is here now. Mickledale was a pre-enclosure hamlet and was first mentioned in 1331.

The course was designed and constructed during 1988 and 1989 by the architect John Day, who had the concept to build a course with holes of varying length and with a degree of difficulty to provide a challenge for every category of golfer. You are welcome to enjoy Frodsham Golf Club either as a member or as a visitor.

It is worth noting the stand of mature oak trees adjacent to the golf course near to the hillfort which denote a pre-enclosure boundary.

Foxhill

Below the Iron Age fort lays an imposing house known as Foxhill. It is possible there was an earlier house on the site in the 1840s known as the Wood House but this has been demolished. This is not shown on the 1846 tithe map which shows the site as a field down to pasture called 'common lot'.

In the 1860s Reverend Richard Greenhall and his brother Sir Gilbert Greenhall of the famous brewing family bought the land off the Marquis of Cholmondeley. A quarry in the hillside was developed as a Japanese-style garden and the house was designed in an Italianate style. Richard went on to become the Archdeacon of Chester in 1866 but died in 1867 before the house was finished.

The unfinished house was bought by James and Mary Reynolds. They were involved in the tannery industry and as leather merchants but James later moved into the sugar industry. They moved into the house in 1870 and it was originally known as 'Woodlands' but the name was changed to Foxhill Hall, possibly as a play on words on the name 'reynard' applied to foxes, and similar to their surname. A folly was built on the hillside and other estate buildings were added. The couple had no children so the house was sold in 1895 to Phillip Speakman.

Phillip and his wife Sarah had made their money from ship building and as coal and lime merchants. Phillip died in 1899 but Sarah continued to live there until 1917. The new owners were Frank and Joan Brocklehurst (1917-1920) who had made their money from ship owning and trading in South America.

In 1920 the property was sold to Robert and Alice Newton Davies who lived there until 1944. Robert was a senior partner in a colliery but also traded in coal, sand, whiting and lime. He died in 1938 but his wife continued to live there with her sister, Miss Lily Hirst during the war before selling the property to Christopher and Coraline Posnett in 1945. Christopher Posnett was also in the tannery industry and was a staunch Methodist. The property was sold to Lawrence and Norah

Pilkington, of the glass manufacturing family, who lived there between 1960 and 1968. The property was generously offered to the Bishop of Chester, Bishop Gerald Ellison, as a Diocesan Conference Centre. The house was refurbished and reopened in 1969, managed by husband and wife wardens

Dr Pilkington had restored the woodlands and developed the arboretum. He brought in many rare trees and shrubs to replace the severe tree felling activities that had occurred during the war. The arboretum was opened to the public in 1994.

Woodland Trust

Much of the hillside is now managed by the Woodland Trust whose objective is to see a country rich in native woods and trees enjoyed and valued by everyone. Their aims are to:
1 Work with others to plant more native trees.
2 Protect native woods, trees and their wildlife for the future.
3 Inspire everyone to enjoy and value woods and trees.

This group of three woods comprises Snidley Moor, Woodhouse Hill and Frodsham Hill Wood. Collectively these sites form the second largest continuous block of broadleaved woodland in the county, offering fantastic views from the Welsh borders to the Western Pennines and Bowland Fells, with over 3km of paths. Each has its own special character, with Snidley Moor, as its name suggests, retaining heather and bilberry indicative of its past history as grazed heath and woodland. Areas of Woodhouse Hill and Frodsham Hill are recorded on the ancient woodland inventory.

Although acquired by the Trust at different times, similarities between the woods and their close proximity allow for an integrated approach to their long term development, for the benefit of both people and wildlife. Access is via a public bridleway from Manley Road. Public footpaths run across the site from east to west, as well as down the eastern boundary. There is a waymarked trail and numerous permissive paths. The organisation replanted a large area of trees in about 2000 and has even included a children's play area with structures loosely based on Iron Age hut circles, just to confuse archaeologists in years to come.

Sand Caves

The geology of the sandstone ridge and around the hillforts was shaped by the ice sheets of the great ice age around 15,000 years ago. This scoured the ground and left deposits of clay, sand and gravel. The action of wind on the exposed cliffs created wind-eroded hollows which can still be seen on the lower parts of the cliffs such as at Woodhouses. Other caves in the area have been dug out to extract the sand which was sold for a variety of purposes such as floor coverings and as a scouring agent. Billy Tweedle was one of the last 'sandmen' in the area. It is possible that the term 'happy as a sand boy' derives from this trade but why they should be happier than anybody else is a mystery.

Sand caves are found at Helsby, the Beeston Grotto, Mad Allen's Hole near Maiden Castle and many other places amongst the sandstone cliffs.

Queen Charlotte's Wood Campsite

The 1839 tithe apportionment for the site of Queen Charlotte's Wood shows it as a woodland plantation owned and occupied by 'the trustees of the late John Arden'. The trustees are listed as Edward Lord Skelmersdale, Wilbraham Edgerton and Randle Egerton. The name 'Queen Charlotte's Wood' first appears on the 1st edition OS map of c.1872. Queen Charlotte, was the wife of King George III (1738-1820) and the grandmother of Queen Victoria. She was directly descended from Margarita de Castro y Sousa, a black branch of the Portuguese Royal House; and she has latterly been heralded as one of the '100 Great Black Britons'.

QCW site before the Scout Camp

Why the site was named as Queen Charlotte's Wood is unknown. Queen Charlotte was a keen amateur botanist and George III had the nickname 'Farmer George' so there may be a clue somewhere there but who knows.

Ian and April Nichols gave us a potted history of Queen Charlotte's Wood (QCW)

Captured Memories across the Hillforts of Cheshire - Woodhouse

Campsite which is situated between Woodhouse and Helsby hillforts.

The campsite covers nearly nine acres and was previously owned by Colonel Robert Stead and in 1963 he gave permission for the scouts to use the area for camping and other outdoor activities. Colonel Stead had been the District Commissioner for NW Cheshire Scouts from 1933 to 1953 and he had often allowed scouts to camp on land around his home on Helsby Hill.

The QCW site was not ideal for camping as it was in a valley completely covered in bracken and with few trees and there was no water supply. So, the first thing the scouts did when they were able to use the land in 1963 was to clear the bracken and make level, grassed areas for pitching tents as well as draining the site and installing a water supply. The work was organised by the then District Commissioner, Harry Woulds and Bob Land took on the job of warden of the site with help from Jack Mather and Mick Huckle. A ex-contractors hut was obtained for £1500 which was formally opened and dedicated to Harry Woulds who died in 1975. Further developments followed with the installation of flush toilets and washing facilities in 1978 with the help of a grant from ICI and Halton Jubilee Fund.

Opening of the Hideaway 1994

In 1984 the Stead family very generously made a gift of the site to NW Cheshire District Scouts and in 1987 April Nichols took over as warden assisted by David McMaster and Vernon Henry. In 1990, April became the District Commissioner and was assisted on the site by her husband Ian.

The next major change was in 1991 when a fund-raising project organised by April to provide roads, lighting, a new hut with sleeping quarters, catering facilities, toilets and hot showers. A total of £133,000 was raised from scout group activities, donations from companies and other organisations. The 'Hideaway', as the building was called, was officially opened in 1994 by the Lord Lieutenant of

Cheshire, William Bromley Davenport.

The site has continued to develop and there are some 4000 stay nights by groups from Cheshire, countrywide and International visitors. Ian and April continue to manage the site with the help of a dedicated team of volunteers.

Mersey View Pleasure Grounds and the Forest Hills Hotel

Increasingly throughout the later 19th century the Frodsham hills became a desirable destination for day trippers from the surrounding conurbations of Liverpool, Manchester, St Helens etc. This was probably accelerated by the arrival of the railway station at Frodsham in 1850, which would have provided previously unprecedented access for the lower classes of society to the rural hinterland of Cheshire.

The Forest Hills Hotel was constructed in 1988 by the current owner, Mr Brian Peck with its superb location on top of Frodsham Hill and wonderful views across the Mersey estuary.

The site had been used as a business for over 100 years and early records show there had been a coffee shop here before the turn of the century. During the early 1900s the business was extended to include further public entertainments such as live music and dancing. The area was ideal for picnic parties, Sunday-school outings and day trippers looking to enjoy the simple pleasures of a children's playground, swing boats and a helter-skelter.

During the Second World War the business ceased whilst the premises were taken over by the Ministry of Defence and the skating rink turned into a hospital. In 1947 the site was returned to the owners and further development of the catering and entertainment facilities took place. After the war and throughout the 1950s there was an upturn in fortunes, people had more money to spend benefiting the leisure business in particular.

The emphasis during the 1960s was placed on the dance hall and live entertainment. In the late 60s early 70s, ballroom dancing gave way to pop groups and cabaret artistes. Many famous artistes who appeared include Gerry and the Pacemakers, the Searchers, Showaddywaddy, Lulu and Luvvers and the swinging Blue Jeans. Undoubtedly the most exciting night of all was in 1963 when the Beatles performed, many local people have vivid memories of the exhilarating atmosphere on that incredible night. The lively programme also included such well known personalities as Bob Monkhouse, Frankie Vaughan, Cannon & Ball, Tom O'Conner and Ken Dodd.

Captured Memories across the Hillforts of Cheshire - Woodhouse

Mersey View Pleasure Grounds, Overton Hill c1955

"I remember going every year to Frodsham with the Orange Lodge. We would play on the helter-skelter and also the swingboats. It was a great day out! I went to a party there the other year at a country club, how it has all changed but the view from the hill is still as good as ever."

Francis Frith

Taken in 1905, this picture shows the Mersey view Pleasure-grounds opened by M Briscoe in 1865. This photograph was taken before the Helter Skelter was built. You can see the Swingboats to the right of the photograph. The buildings have been converted by the current Mersey View nightclub and most of what you see is now the Mersey View car park.

40

Captured Memories across the Hillforts of Cheshire - Woodhouse

Mrs. Parker Hoose had the helter-skelter built in 1908 at a cost of £300. It was demolished in 1977.

References:
1. Sandstone Trail Walkers Guide, Cheshire West and Chester
2. Dunsdale Hollow: Frodsham History Society Journal, Issue 25, 1998
3. 'Frodsham in the War Years' produced by the Frodsham and District local history group.
4. www.frodshamgolf.co.uk
5. Foxhill: Frodsham and District Local History Journal, Issues 21 and 22.

Captured Memories across the Hillforts of Cheshire

Artist's impression of Eddisbury Hillfort by Dai Owen

Archaeological dig of the entrance way in 2010

LIDAR view of Eddisbury – see page xi

EDDISBURY HILLFORT

43

Eddisbury

The view from the top

There is increasing evidence that Eddisbury Hill has been a centre for habitation ranging from Neolithic, through the Bronze and Iron ages to Roman and Medieval activity. The Roman Watling Street from Manchester to Chester passed to the south of the hill and its line can still be traced. There was an excavation in Nettleford Wood near Organsdale Farm by E Kirk in 1885, re-examined in 1950 and further studies made by A.C and E Waddelove in 1982. This study cast some doubt on whether what was found was Roman. The excavation revealed a structure that was not typical of Roman roads and may have been altered in medieval times. The excavation was filled in to protect the structure.

In 1870-72, John Marius Wilson's 'Imperial Gazetteer of England and Wales' described Eddisbury like this: "A township and a hundred in Cheshire. The township is in Delamere parish, and lies in Delamere forest, 7½ miles SW of Northwich. It covers 3,890 acres with a population of 228 and 41 houses. It was known to the Saxons as Eadersbyrig; it had a fortification belonging to Ethelfleda, and now occupied by a lodge; and it gives the title of baron to the Stanleys of Alderley." A 'hundred' was a division of a County in England originally supposed to contain a hundred families.

The parish is still fairly sparsely populated and spread over a wide area. Below the hill, the area is mainly agricultural but in some parts is being taken over by sand quarrying. A number of large sand quarries such as the Fourways Sand Quarry owned by Tilcon are wet-workings and are now flooded. The lake from which the village of Oakmere takes its name is a site of scientific interest and is located to the southeast of the hill. There is another Iron Age enclosure in the area at Oakmere (Map Ref: SJ576678) which is not part of the Habitats and Hillforts programme. This site was defended by a single bank and external ditch, stands on a promontory of sand and gravel to the east of Oakmere. The settlement was protected on three sides by water, with only the neck needing defences. In prehistoric times the bank would have stretched right up to the water, but evidence indicates that water levels have dropped since then as there is now a slight gap to the north. A causeway breaks the ditch almost halfway along.

Don Wilson, a local resident, told us that the development of the Eddisbury area owes much to the building of Delamere Station around the 1860s. This was a major employer having a Station Master and clerks. There was an extensive array of goods sheds which went in the 1960s. In the early days, farming relied on the service to transport potatoes and milk to Manchester and bringing excursions from Liverpool and Manchester to explore the countryside. A recent initiative between the Forestry Commission and Northern Rail is aimed to encourage visitors to the Delamere Forest and attractions such as the aerial adventure route, 'Go-Ape', has been constructed as well as cycle tracks and cycle hire. Visitor numbers are hard to estimate but it is thought that the forest now attracts as many visitors as Chester Zoo.

For about the last ten years, Eddisbury Hill has reverberated to a different sound. Near to the Visitors' Centre in Delamere forest is an open-air concert venue and is getting quite a reputation with Jools Holland, The Sugarbabes, Status Quo and others, all performing here over the last few years. As an open air venue, Delamere is an impressive location and has been quite successful since the concerts were first organised.

The Marley Tile Factory started production in the 1950s and was situated below the hill to the north. There were three production lines, one automatic, two semi-automatic; one line were used only intermittently utilising the machine crew operating one of the other lines; capacity was operating at 12 million plain plus 9 million large tiles or 16 million large tiles. If the third line was fully operated on a single shift the capacity would be increased by 12 million plain tiles. Profiles produced were the plain, feature, Ludlow Major, Modern and Wessex tiles. The factory closed in 2007 but the site is huge and has an old quarry and lake behind the buildings.

Adjacent to the old Marley Tile factory sits the Delamere Forest Golf Club which was born in 1910. It is a natural heathland course, despite the word Forest, but trees do form part of its defence on several holes and there are a number of blind drives, some involving a long carry. Both the ninth and the 18th dog-leg around a central wood and call for tee shots over "out of bounds" and the 15th hole is a dog-leg left with a blind drive over a hill again with an out of bounds. The opening five holes will stretch any player and there are many more holes with character but the fifth is a real test with a long uphill carry to the green, with a pond to the left and below the green.

To the east of the summit are the remains of a sandstone quarry which is reputed to have supplied stone for the Vale Royal Abbey, Beeston Castle, Abbey Arms and Delamere School. The site is now occupied by the Eddisbury Hill Park which started just after the Second World War as a holiday park before becoming a residential, park homes, site in the late 1960s. Across the road is the Delamere Grove park homes site which occupies the main part of the quarry and where the quarry offices were situated.

Captured Memories across the Hillforts of Cheshire - Eddisbury

The present Delamere Forest is the remnant of the Forests of Mara and Mondrem, which covered over 60 square miles (160 km^2) in the north-west of the county in the 11th century. This was a hunting forest of the Norman Earls of Chester, it was subject to the harsh forest law, which greatly limited agricultural use for centuries. Ownership passed to the Crown in 1812 and then to the Forestry Commission (established in 1919) in 1924, which now manages the forest. The forest covers some 2,400 acres and includes two Forestry Commission Nurseries at Abbots Moss producing 6 million seedling trees annually. In 1987 a large cache of IRA weapons was discovered by the police, concealed near to the switchback road.

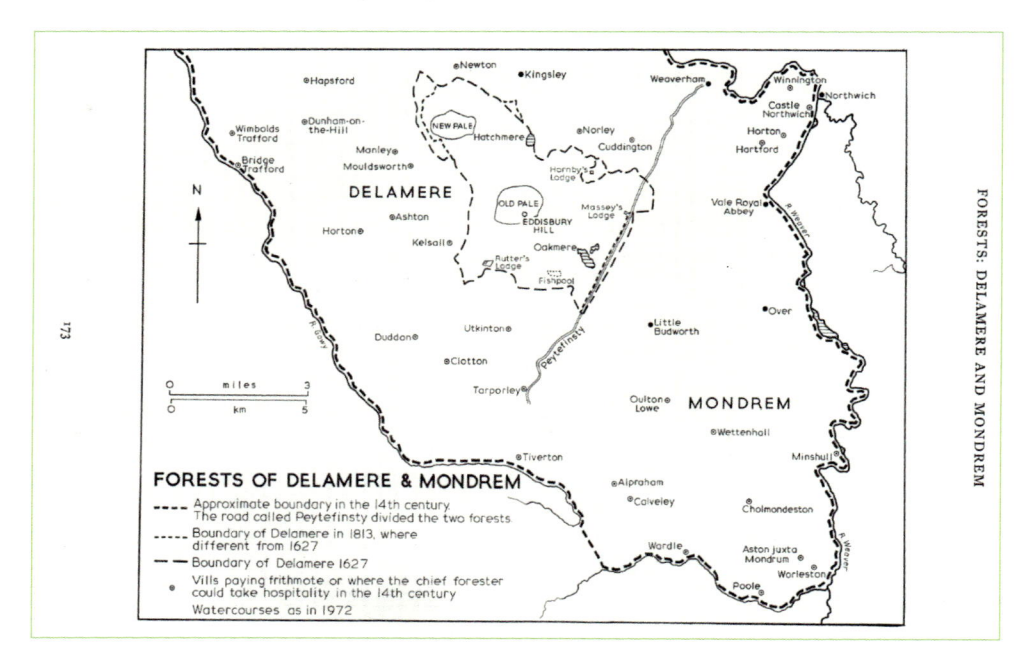

FORESTS OF DELAMERE & MONDREM
- - - - Approximate boundary in the 14th century. The road called Peytefinsty divided the two forests
- - - - - Boundary of Delamere in 1813, where different from 1627
——— Boundary of Delamere 1627
• Vills paying frithmote or where the chief forester could take hospitality in the 14th century
Watercourses as in 1972

The Old Pale hill (176 metres, SJ543696) stands towards the south of the Forestry Commission-owned area; it forms the high point of the northern mass of the Mid Cheshire Ridge. The summit, Pale Heights, has a trig point and three transmitter masts which carry radio, television and telephone signals. The masts have been used for police communications but more recently some pods have been leased to mobile telephone operators. The 'Eiffel' type tower was built in 1976 and is 200 ft high. There is an underground complex there which was used for civil defence cold war communications operations. The grassy mound and ventilation shafts can be seen but the site was moth-balled in 1992. The hill was once crowned with a 50 foot-high watch tower to check for fires in the Delamere Forest. A water reservoir was constructed under the hill in 1988 by the North West Water Authority taking water from Lake Vyrnwy in Wales and the River Dee.

A newly constructed view point was opened in November 2009 and consists of a central mound with stones encircling it. The stones came from the eight 'traditional' counties that can be seen from the viewpoint: Cheshire, Derbyshire, Lancashire, Yorkshire, Shropshire and Staffordshire in England, and Denbighshire and Flintshire in Wales. Other municipal areas can also be seen.

The prominent position of the hillforts still has the same draw and 'magical' feel as was probably felt by our Iron Age ancestors. Don Wilson said "I will always remember the turn of the century, and the millennium, spent on the top of Eddisbury Hill. We went to a lovely church service at St Peter's and then, just after midnight, we spent some time with our neighbours on the hillfort watching the distant firework displays throughout Cheshire, fortified with some hot toddies. It was a happy time despite the mud. Another occasion was the total eclipse of the sun on 11th August 1999. Where else would you go to soak up the atmosphere than on the hillfort of Eddisbury? It was a warm, quiet day, and as the eclipse began and the light began to fail, the temperature dropped and a sudden breeze rustled the new corn on the hill. Save for the wind, it was very still and quiet in the gathering gloom. I kept thinking about how our Iron Age forefathers would have interpreted the eclipse. It remains an eerie but very 'warm' experience." This eclipse was about 90% of total as viewed in Cheshire and was similar to the last 'total' one on the 29th June 1927. The next one of this magnitude will not be until 2090.

To the south east of the fort, St Peter's church was built in a clearing in the forest by John Gunnery and was consecrated in 1816. John Gunnery was a stonemason from Liverpool with land and a quarry in Kelsall. The church is in a Gothic Revival style and seats 150 people.

Delamere School

Below the hill lies the Delamere C of E Academy School that was the Delamere County Primary School. Built in 1846, it was once called Forest School but more commonly known as Delamere National School. It is an imposing building for a rural community in a 'gothic' style and cost £1500 to build, raised by subscription. It could hold 200 pupils but in 1860 the attendance was 95. By the turn of the century the numbers were around 120 drawn from Oakmere, Delamere and Eddisbury. A fair was held on Old Pale Heights to raise money for the building of the school house in 1880.

Captured Memories across the Hillforts of Cheshire - Eddisbury

Delamere School c. 1846 (from an engraving)

Robin Ackerley was born in the schoolhouse and has returned to live in the area. His father, Norman, was headmaster of the school in 1935, at the young age of 26. He later moved to Weaverham Secondary Modern School and Robin's mother, Nancy, took over as headmistress in 1954 until 1970. Other heads have been Peter Bowyer, Mrs Mary Carter and the current head, Steve Docking. The school was classed as a Grade II listed building in April 1986. The picture shows a Delamere school trip to Eddisbury Hill in the 1950s with the headmaster, Norman Ackerley.

Robin told us that the school cook and caretaker, Lydia Robinson, prepared meals for over 80 children in a kitchen that was 7 feet square at a charge of 2d (old pence) per head. This continued between 1937 and 1948 when the kitchen was extended. It was thought to be particularly important that the children received a good meal as many came from relatively poor farming families. The wartime Ministry of Food was particularly impressed and the Delamere School canteen became the model for the scheme for the national provision of school dinners.

Robin Ackerley and schoolchildren on Eddisbury Hill in the 1950s.

The current headmaster, Steve Docking explained that the school bell was last rung on VE day 1945 by Tommy Craven. Due to the excitement of the end of the war he rang the bell so hard that it fell off the roof! The bell has sat in school since that day gathering dust.

Steve told us that "The school and community decided that to open the new Academy we should launch a campaign to have the bell resurrected. The bell went on tour to many places of work; t-shirts were produced to commemorate this. We were also visited by Granada Reports who ran a feature, this resulted in a £1000 donation by a gentleman who had no association with the school but was moved by our story. Over the course of three months our bell appeal raised over £6000 and as result of this we were able to restore it fully to its rightful home.

School Dinners

On the 26th April 2011 our new Academy officially opened. We had several hundred people in attendance, past pupils, present pupils, parents and members of our community. The 'piéce de résistance' was that Tommy Craven, now approaching his 80th year, returned to school and rang the bell again for the first time since he broke it 66 years earlier.

Small rural schools are an important part of the cultural make up of our society and it is important that we aim to preserve our history and make them special for all members of the community. The bell project is just one example of what makes The Delamere C of E Academy a special place to learn."

School Bell

Captured Memories across the Hillforts of Cheshire - Eddisbury

Delamere Academy 2011

William J Varley and the excavation of Castle Ditch, Eddisbury

Professor William J Varley undertook a programme of excavation on Eddisbury Hill in three successive seasons during the Long Vacations of 1936 to 1938 under the auspices of the 'Bickerton Camp Scheme'. William Varley was a Professor in the Department of Geography at the University of Liverpool during the 1930s and he had embarked on "the systematic excavation of the hillforts of Cheshire" with work at Maiden Castle, Bickerton between 1932 and 1935. He had rapidly realised that he could not undertake "worth-while excavations of hill-forts with such a small labour force" (namely half a dozen students from his own Department at the University); and he had the idea of recruiting labour from the clubs for the unemployed being run by the Liverpool Occupational Centres Committee. The arrangement was that volunteers from the clubs would give their labour to Varley between 8:30 am and 1 pm each working day for which they were fed, clothed and housed (additionally they could still draw their benefits under the several schemes for the unemployed). The volunteers were supervised by a number of qualified archaeologists under the direction of William Varley himself. This arrangement was started at Maiden Castle and proved such a success that it was rolled on to the excavations at Eddisbury.

The Chamber in the Forest

During the medieval period it became increasingly common for hunting to take place in deer parks and there are two former sites on the sandstone ridge which are identified by the place names Old Pale on Eddisbury Hill and New Pale about 3 miles to the northwest near to Manley Common.

The Old Pale is the area immediately around Eddisbury Hill and is an enclosed tract of the Royal Forest of Mara (now Delamere). It was enclosed in 1237 by John Done. It should be noted that the term 'forest' meant an area of wooded, or open, countryside that fell under forest law and not just a heavily wooded area as we know it today. The forests were owned by the King and were preserved for the hunting of deer which were a significant source of meat at this time. They were also a valuable source of income to the crown as licences were granted to wealthy landowners for the creation of deer parks. This partly explains why there are so few centres of habitation in the vicinity and the straightness of many of the roads. The New Pale was enclosed in the 17th Century and was surrounded by a low stone wall.

Eddisbury Hill lay in the heart of the Forest of Delamere and was from the 14th century the site of a forest lodge, known as 'the Chamber in the Forest'. The lodge was the residence of the chief keepers of the forest, the Done family and their descendants, the Ardernes, until the enclosure of the Forest of Delamere in 1812. There are a number of references to repairs and rebuilding of the forest lodge from the 15th to 17th centuries. Local legend has it that there was a murder at the lodge and that the blood continued to seep from the hearthstone and that was why the lodge was dismantled.

The enclosure of the Delamere forest was finally completed in 1819. Agricultural and was enclosed, creating the pattern of small to medium (up to 8ha) regular fields with straight hawthorn hedgerows. In the southern areas enclosure and forestry were also occurring, but on a significantly smaller scale. These areas were also subject to change by the activities of the local estates to improve their agricultural land.

Varley's excavations in 1936 uncovered the remains of the forest lodge buildings and he has suggested a sequence of occupation from 1350 to 1800. The lodge was confined to a small area at the south-east corner of the fort, described on the OS First Edition 6": 1 mile map as 'Merrick's Hill or the Chamber' (John Merrick was the last tenant of the lodge). There had been a limited investigation by a geologist, John Edwards, about 8-9 years ago but his findings are poorly recorded. The site was being investigated by Liverpool University in August 2010.

Peter Powell remembers a post-war dig at Eddisbury. He reckons it was in 1946 or 1947. He was at Delamere School then (about 12-years old as he is 76 this year) and walked each day over the hill from Station Road to school and back home. He is pretty sure it wasn't during the war years and he would have left school around 15. He remembers the dig being visible from Eddisbury Hill Road so it could have been the Merricks Hill part but he seemed to think it was further west than this. He said that the school kids were shown some pottery from the dig which may suggest the hunting lodge site.

Don Wilson, a local resident, told of a tunnel about 20 yds long which was probably a culvert of the old lodge. He said it was a 'rite of passage' for local youths to crawl through this cramped tunnel.

Wartime Activities

Eddisbury Hill was frequently crossed by bombers on route to Liverpool and it is said that decoy lights were deployed on the hill to confuse the enemy. The hill had search lights on it between 1939 and 1945. Charles Ashbrook was killed by a bomb in 1941 when on his way to join his wife in the three air-raid shelters at Delamere School. His grandsons still live in the area.

Robin Ackerley told us that about 500 incendiary bombs and a land mine were dropped on a field near to the fort. His anecdote illustrates the seriousness and sometimes comic nature of the time. "My Dad was the local Air Raid Precautions (ARP) warden and as you know Delamere, and Eddisbury Hill in particular, was badly affected by the air raids intended for Liverpool. The 28th November 2010 will be the 70th anniversary of the night this area suffered its heaviest bombardment; and several places were known to have been hit, including the cottages where our bungalow now stands and the house in Utkinton where my grandmother was born. One night, Dad was out on patrol when there came a knock at the door. Mum answered it; it was a neighbour who worked on the local farm. He asked if Dad was in; Mum said he wasn't but, it being a cold night, invited him in. He came in and stood by the fire near to where I was lying in my carrycot. "What can I do for you?" asked Mum. Our visitor fished inside his coat. "I've brewt him one o' these 'ere insanitary bombs," he announced proudly, producing one of the many incendiaries that had fallen on the area the night before, some of which had failed to go off. Forgetting any rules of hospitality Mum grabbed hold of our visitor and virtually threw him out of the door. And so I lived to tell the tale….."

Evacuees from Manchester and Liverpool were housed on Organsdale Farm and elsewhere in the area.

Captured Memories across the Hillforts of Cheshire - Eddisbury

Eddisbury Hill Farm is said to have hosted a prisoner-of-war camp for Italian Officers during the World War II, many of whom worked on the land during their time there. The camp was situated near to the water tower on the farm. There were about 20 prisoner-of-war camps in Cheshire. An American forces base was also said to be on the farm.

Eddisbury Hill as photographed by the RAF in 1947. PoW huts and three search light batteries are shown behind Eddisbury Hill Farm (bottom right)

A badge was found by a metal detector in the field behind Eddisbury Hill Farm in 2010. It is the Luftwaffe version of an Anti-Aircraft Combat Badge (Flak-Kampfabzeichen Der Luftwaffe). The badge was awarded after accruing 16 points, the equivalent of shooting down 5 enemy planes. Presumably it was dropped by one of the prisoners of war working on the farm.

The Badge found in 2010

53

Local farms and Houses

Old Pale Cottages were built in the 1880s. Thirteen children were raised at one time in number 5! The other row of cottages along this lane was built in 1940 to replace those damaged by bombs during the war.

Eddisbury Hill Farm, immediately east of the fort, has been in existence for a long time. At one time it was a dairy farm owned by Mr Maddock. The farm was bought by Wilfrid Platt in 1942 and is currently owned by his son, Mike Platt. The family owned a fruit and vegetable business in Northwich and the plan was to develop the farm as a fruit growing business but the land proved to be too exposed for this and is mainly arable and potatoes nowadays. During the war the steep slopes of the hillfort ramparts were ploughed and cultivated as part of the 'dig for victory' campaign to increase home-grown food production. The water tower on the farm was built in the 1930s and stored water pumped from a source near to the Delamere Community Centre.

Old Pale Farm, which lies immediately west of the earthworks dates from between 1819 and 1874, when it appears on the First Edition OS map. It is said that there was a royal visit to the farm by Queen Victoria's son. The farm was owned by the Frith family for 5 generations. It was a prosperous farm with dairy cows and sheep and once said to be highest cultivated land in Cheshire. David Frith sold the farm about 8 years ago and moved to Wales. The farm and barns were converted into housing. Most of the land was sold to the Forestry Commission and some 340 acres of trees have been planted on the Old Pale.

A mulberry tree was planted at the Old Pale by James 1 in 1617 to promote the production of local silk but was of the wrong type. It later blew down. Norman Frith is said to have written to the queen to obtain a replacement and this was planted in about 1961. There must be some doubt about this story. Although mulberry trees are used as the food source for silk moths in other parts of the world, the UK silk moth (the silk is actually produced by the caterpillar of the Emperor Moth – *Saturinia pavonia*) is a poor producer of silk and likely to be very inefficient. There was a small-scale silk farm in Hertfordshire where Lady Hart-Dyke produced about 20 lbs of silk a week from 21 acres of mulberry bushes in the 1930s.

Marl Pits

In the centre of the Eddisbury site is the remains of a quarry or marl pit – opinions vary as to its exact definition. It is more likely to have been dug to extract the stone but may have been to reach the underlying marl. Marling of the fields of the Old

Pale, Delamere Lodge and Organsdale Farm was highly successful in the 1850s.

The general definition of marling is using any subsoil, which is different to the topsoil, as a fertilizer and to put 'body' into the soil. In the early 1880s marling was considered as one of the most important Cheshire manures to improve soil fertility. Marl is a natural geological deposit of clay with a high percentage of lime (up to 15%). It is obtained from boulder clay, Keuper marls and from the beds of loam associated with the Keuper sandstone. All these are widely distributed over the county particularly to the west of the ridge. When applied to agricultural land, marl has chemical and physical benefits. On sandy soils, such as here, it improves water retention and adds mineral and organic components. The lime counteracts the acidity of certain soils. The use of marl by the Celtic tribes in Britain was described by Pliny the Elder in A.D. 70 but became widespread in the 12th century. Marling lapsed in the 1800s due to the increased use of bone meal, ash and guano and later by chemical fertilizers and lime.

Marl pits are typically steep sided but with one or more ramps for access by carts and are frequently found in the middle of fields to minimize cartage. The marl will be covered by a layer of top soil which has to be removed before the marl is dug.

References:
1. 'Delamere' The Local History Group 1991, Herald Printers (Whitchurch) Ltd. ISBN 0 9518292 0 3 (Hardback). Research Organiser and Editor Frank A Latham.
2. Delamere School: 'The Story of Kelsall' Elspeth Thomas, Masons Design and Print, Chester
3. Silk worms: 'Bugs Britannica' Peter Marren and Richard Mabey, Chatto and Windus 2010, ISBN 9780701181802
4. Marl pits: Frodsham History Society Journal, Issue 36, 2006.
5. Marl pits: Cheshire Life June 1959, p 43.

Captured Memories across the Hillforts of Cheshire

Artist's impression of Kelsborrow Castle by Dai Owen

Kelsborrow, 2010

LIDAR view of Kelsborrow – see page xi

KELSBORROW CASTLE

57

Kelsborrow Castle

Although there are over 1300 hill forts in England, they are concentrated in south-western England, and there are only seven in Cheshire. Along with Eddisbury and Oakmere, Kelsborrow forms a small cluster of Iron Age forts within 3 miles (5 km) of each other, near the Mouldsworth Gap, a break in the central ridge that runs north–south through Cheshire. This pass was most probably an almost impassable defile until the Romans cut their Watling Street around AD49. The forts at Eddisbury and Oakmere lie to the north-east and east respectively. Oakmere is not a hillfort but is more correctly described as a promontory fort jutting into the mere (see page 44).

Kelsborrow Castle is located at grid reference SJ53176752, 400 ft (120 m) above sea level. The site overlooks the Cheshire Plain to the west, south-west, and south. There is high ground immediately to the east of Kelsborrow Castle, rising to a height of 500 ft (150 m). Kelsborrow Castle is a type of promontory fort, as it exploits the natural steep slopes of the area to create a defensive site. The site is surrounded by an artificial bank and ditch, although there is a gap in the ditch for around 400 ft (120 m) in the west. This is probably because the ground slopes sharply away where there is no ditch. The best surviving parts of the bank are 6 ft (1.8 m) high, and the distance between the outer edge of the ditch and the inner edge of the rampart is 100 ft (30 m). The defences cover 1.75 acres (0.71 ha), and enclose an area of 7.25 acres (2.93 ha). The entrance of the fort is probably in the south-east. The fort was a well-known landmark in the 17th and 18th centuries but farming practices over the years have destroyed most of the earthworks.

The only Bronze Age artefact from Kelsborrow is a bronze palstave axe found in 1810.

The views from the top cross the Mersey and Dee estuaries of the Cheshire plain rimmed by the Peckforton Hills to the south, the Clwydian range to the west with the high point of Moel Fammau. To the south the Long Mynd in Shropshire may be seen on clear days.

There is a public footpath running from The Waste to Boothsdale which passes by the hillfort but visitors should respect that the hillfort is on private farmland belonging to Michael Hardy.

The Early History of 'Castle Hill' Kelsborrow

Dan Garner supplied information on some of the earlier history of the site.

The earliest map to show the residence known as 'Castle Hill' is the 1st edition OS map of 1873; no tithe map exists for Delamere parish and the earliest detailed map of the area is the enclosure map of 1819 which shows the site of 'Castle Hill' as an open field. The Delamere Parish Church was classed as a Crown Church and was outside the jurisdiction of the Bishop of Chester. The rector would have been appointed by the Queen.

The origins of the Castle Hill buildings are not easy to elucidate and to a certain extent it can only be achieved by some old fashioned sleuthing; logically this has involved working backwards in time from a known point in the property's history. In this case the known point is the sale by auction of an estate including 'Castle Hill' on Wednesday 4th October 1933 by John Whittaker Kenworthy. The auction included a booklet detailing how the estate was broken up for the auction and how these parcels had been acquired by the Kenworthy family. In particular there are details of the purchase of 'Castle Hill' by John's father, George Henry Kenworthy, from Henry Hall, Hannah Rowe Hall and Margaret Louisa Beard in 1892.

The 1891 census return shows that 'Castle Hill' was occupied by a John Joseph Beard and his wife Margaret (quite probably the Margaret Louisa Beard mentioned in 1892); John Joseph Beard is listed as being born in Buenos Aries (Argentina) in about 1855, whilst Margaret was born in Ashton-Under-Lyne (Lancashire) in about 1856. John Joseph Beard is listed as a 'farmer' by profession but the presence of three servants in the household suggests a certain level of affluence so perhaps a 'gentleman farmer' is more appropriate. What is not clear is whether or not John actually owned 'Castle Hill' or simply resided there.

It was not possible to locate any information for the 1881 census but the 1871 census shows that 'Castle Hill' was occupied by Henry Hall and his wife Hannah (presumably the Henry Hall and Hannah Rowe Hall mentioned in 1892). Henry Hall is listed as being born in Ashton-Under-Lyne (Lancashire) in about 1815, whilst Hannah was born in Measham (Derbyshire) in about 1828. Henry is listed as a solicitor by profession but it is also stated that he was 'blind' by 1871 so presumably he had other strings to his bow? The only other resident of the house is listed as a servant called Martha Bouder. The 1st edition OS map of 1873 shows 'Castle Hill' as a large house with numerous outbuildings and large formal gardens suggestive of a fairly grand residence. It is hard to be certain but it seems likely that there is some family link between the Halls and the Beards (both Henry Hall and Margaret Beard were born in Ashton-Under-Lyne); and perhaps Margaret was a Hall (maybe even Henry and Hannah's daughter) prior to her marriage to John Beard?

The 1861 census refers to the property as 'Castle Hill Farm' and states that it was occupied by a James McNulty who was born in Ireland about 1816 and is listed as a 'joiner' by profession. The only other occupant present was a Samuel Bradley who is listed as a 'border'. This certainly suggests that between 1861 and 1871 there was a shift in the class of the residents at 'Castle Hill'; perhaps a remodelling of the site took place during the decade resulting in a change of use from a working farm to a stylish country residence.

Kelsborrow Estate

The creation of the Kenworthy Estate at Kelsborrow was begun by George Henry Kenworthy when he acquired 'Castle Hill' in 1892.

View from Kelsborrow Castle 1933 – note the Shire Horses in the foreground.

A trawl of the 1901 census returns revealed that George Henry Kenworthy was residing at Hurst Hall, Hurst (Ashton-Under-Lyne, Lancashire) on the night of the census with his son John W Kenworthy and 5 servants (including a house keeper, cook, house maid, waitress and kitchen maid). The 1901 census also reveals that on the night the only residents of 'Castle Hill' were 2 servants and a visitor; suggesting that this was very much a secondary residence for the Kenworthy family. In 1901 George Henry Kenworthy was listed as a cotton manufacturer and Kelly's Directory of Hurst for 1905 lists George and his son John as local JPs; so the Kenworthy family were clearly of some standing in the local community of Hurst.

Further scrutiny of the census returns between 1851 and 1881 reveals some additional insights into the rise of the Kenworthy dynasty. It would appear that in 1851 George Kenworthy was living in a cottage with his widowed mother and 6 other family members; his mother was engaged as a house-keeper whilst the rest of the family worked in the cotton industry variously engaged as spinners, frame tenters and, lowliest of all, George who was a 'cotton piecer' (or scavenger). Ten years later George (born 1835) had progressed to become a cotton spinner; however, more significantly he had married Sarah Anne Whittaker (born 1833) in 1859 who was the only daughter of John Whittaker a local cotton manufacturer. The Whittaker's were clearly an important family in the area as the local church of St. John included a private chapel erected by Oldham Whittaker prior to his death in 1871. It is perhaps for this reason that George thought it prudent to name his son John Whittaker Kenworthy (born in 1861) certainly by 1881 George had progressed from 'cotton spinner' to 'cotton manufacturer', residing at Hurst Hall and with 5 domestic servants in his household. The Kenworthy Estate Office is shown as at 166 Stamford Street, Stalybridge. It is probable that the Castle Hill Estate was used as their country retreat.

The Kenworthy's only began their estate building in 1892 and the layout of the buildings has been referred to as a Cheshire Model Farm. The concept of a model farm was an 18th-19th century experimental farm, which researched and demonstrated improvements in agricultural techniques, efficiency, and building layout. Education and commitment to improving welfare standards of workers were also aspects of the ideal farm movement. Farm buildings were designed to be beautiful as well as utilitarian. The farm and buildings were certainly of a very high quality. They were brick built and the architecture of the buildings is thought to be very similar to others in Cheshire. The Castle Hill residence had 8 bedrooms and was set in 250 acres of estate.

Castle Hill Residence in 1933 – note the range of carefully managed hollies

Captured Memories across the Hillforts of Cheshire - Kelsborrow

STUD FARM—GROUP OF BUILDINGS

John Kenworthy is said to have been somewhat eccentric and had a great interest in Shire horses. The farm was an important stud farm and was home to many of the leading shire horses of the country. The attention to detail can be seen in the stables and the walls that delineated the paddocks for the horses. The hedges of the paddocks are grown on dressed stone walls and each paddock was double fenced and provided with a water supply and boxes for the horses. In the late 19th and early 20th century Shire Horses were in high demand as draught animals for both agricultural and industrial sectors as well as playing an important role in WWI pulling heavy artillery for the military.

A study of changes to the layout of 'Castle Hill' between 1873 and 1898 suggests that there were some attempts made to 'gentrify' the landscape. Most significantly the formal gardens appear to have been extended to the south and west where they were delimited by a stone built 'ha-ha' furnished with semi-circular 'bastions' at the corners. Whilst to the south of the residence at Birch Hill a semi-circular folly had also appeared by 1898 (marked on the map as 'stand'); only the base of this now remains but it may have originally functioned as a viewing tower. It is likely

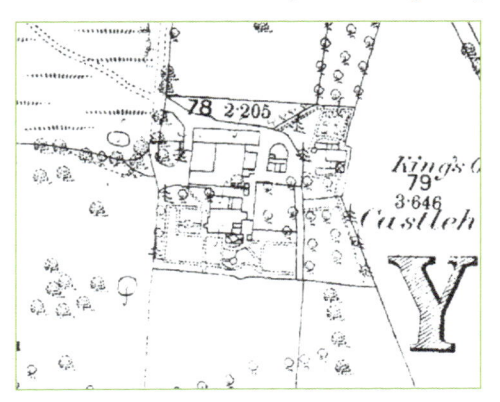

'Castle Hill' c.1873

'Castle Hill' c.1898

that these alterations were part of the development of the landscape as part of the new 'Kenworthy Estate'.

By 1933 the house was laid out with about 5 acres of gardens including a magnificent double sided herbaceous border that stretched for some 100 yards. At the end of the border

Current view of 'Castle Hill' looking east and the 'ha-ha' built in c 1890s.

there was a 300 foot-deep well, said to have been dug by Welsh miners. The water was raised by a windmill and fed into a large (35,000 gallon), tiled underground storage tank. The gardens had a fine collection of around 600 holly trees and it was claimed to contain specimens of every known variety. It is said that John Kenworthy insisted that these trees and shrubs were beautifully manicured to such an extent that no leaf was to be cut across but the whole leaf removed! Gardeners were employed solely for this task.

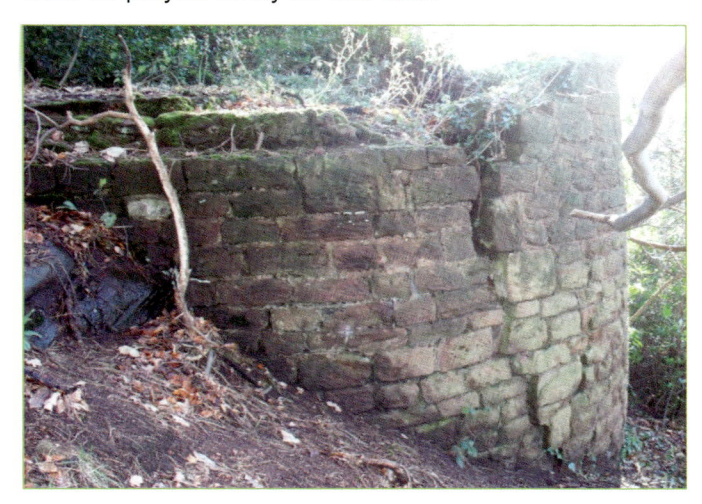

One feature of the farm was said to be the pond surrounded by 7 pine trees to act as a landmark for a water supply that could be used by drovers in the past. The pond at The Waste was likely to have been a marl pit or a small quarry.

A local newsletter of uncertain origin and date gives an account of life on the Kenworthy

The remains of the folly 'stand' built around the 1890s

estate but the copy we have seen is incomplete. It says that the overall control of the estate was by the bailiff, James Cliffe. There were 12 stud shire horses at any one time. Castle Hill was somewhat notorious for the number of suicides which took place over the years – a man hung himself in the bailiff's coach house; a man drowned himself in a pond near the marl pit; James Woodcock drowned himself in the Castle Yard pit and a girl called Rimmer drowned herself in the Folly Field pit. The author of the article went on to say that he left Castle Hill in March 1917 and went to work for Brummer, Mond and Co at Winnington.

The Hardy family

The current farming family, Mike, his wife Claire and his aunt Joan Hardy, provided a fascinating insight into the history of the farm.

Mike Hardy has in his possession the sale booklet for the estate which relates to his grandparents purchase of the farm in 1933. The estate included Castle Hill Farm, Harewood Hill Farm and Delamere Farm as well as a number of other dwellings. It provides an insight into a number of local residents at the time.

> **Booklet detailing the particulars of sale by private auction for 'An Attractive Freehold Residential and Agricultural Estate with stud farm, Kelsall, Nr. Chester'.**
>
> Sold by John Whittaker Kenworthy – auction at 3pm on Wednesday 4th October 1933.
>
> Within the conditions of sale is the following information detailing the parcels of land that were purchased to make the estate
>
> THE TITLE SHALL COMMENCE:—
> (i) As to part of the property being the plots of land shown on the sale plan and numbered respectively 455, 456, 452, 448, 451, 450, 457, 424, 427, 392, 393, 394, 391, 3913, 378, 379, 321, 320, 319, 425, 398, 422, 399, 400, 401, 416 and 417 including the dwellinghouse known as "Castle Hill" and the out buildings and grounds occupied therewith erected on the said plot and numbered 451 and the other buildings erected on certain other of the said plots or on some part thereof with a Conveyance dated the 3ist day of October 1892 and made between Henry Hall of the first part Margaret Louisa Beard of the second part Hannah Rowe Hall of the third part and George Henry Kenworthy (the father of the Vendor) of the fourth part.

(ii) As to another part of the property known as "Booth Dale" being the plots numbered 397, 396 and 375 on the sale plan and the cottage erected on some part of the said plot numbered 375 with a Conveyance dated the 23rd day of November 1892 and made between Thomas Astbury of the one part and the said George Henry Kenworthy of the other part.

(iii) As to the plots of land numbered 458, 488, 4883, 487, 489 and 497 including the cottages (now known as "Delamere Farm Cottages") and other buildings erected thereon with the Conveyance to the Vendor dated the 1st day of May 1896 and made between Thomas Hall and Frank Morrey of the first part Mary Morrey of the second part and the Vendor of the third part.

(iv) As to the plots numbered 524 and 526 on the sale plan and the two cottages erected thereon with the said Conveyance of the 1st day of May 1896.

(v) As to the major portion of the plot numbered 534 on the sale plan with the Conveyance of the same to the Vendor dated the 20th day of July 1906 and made between Mary Needham Robert Needham John Windsor Needham and Edward Rushton Needham of the one part and the Vendor of the other part.

(vi) As to the remaining portion of the said plot numbered 534 and as to the plot numbered 533 and cottage known as "Hollybank" with the conveyance of the same to the Vendor dated the 29th day of September 1899 and made between Thomas Ward and John Weston of the one part and the Vendor of the other part.

(vii) As to the plots of land numbered 531, 532, 527, 528, 493, 494, 495, 496, 490, 491, 492, 446 and 447 on the sale plan with the Conveyance thereof to the Vendor dated the 1st day of March 1899 and made between the Revd. Samuel Ward Payne of the one part and the Vendor of the other part.

(viii) As to the plots of land numbered 390, 380/388/389 and 275 and the dwellinghouse known as "Summer Bank" with the Conveyance thereof to the Vendor dated the 21st day of January 1905 and made between James Griffiths of the one part and the Vendor of the other part.

(ix) As to all that part of the property which is coloured blue and yellow on the sale plan with the Conveyance thereof to the Vendor dated the 30th day of December 1922 and made between John Stringer Walker of the first part Henry Richard Walker of the second part the said Henry Richard Walker and Joseph Langton Hewer of the third part and the Vendor of the fourth part.

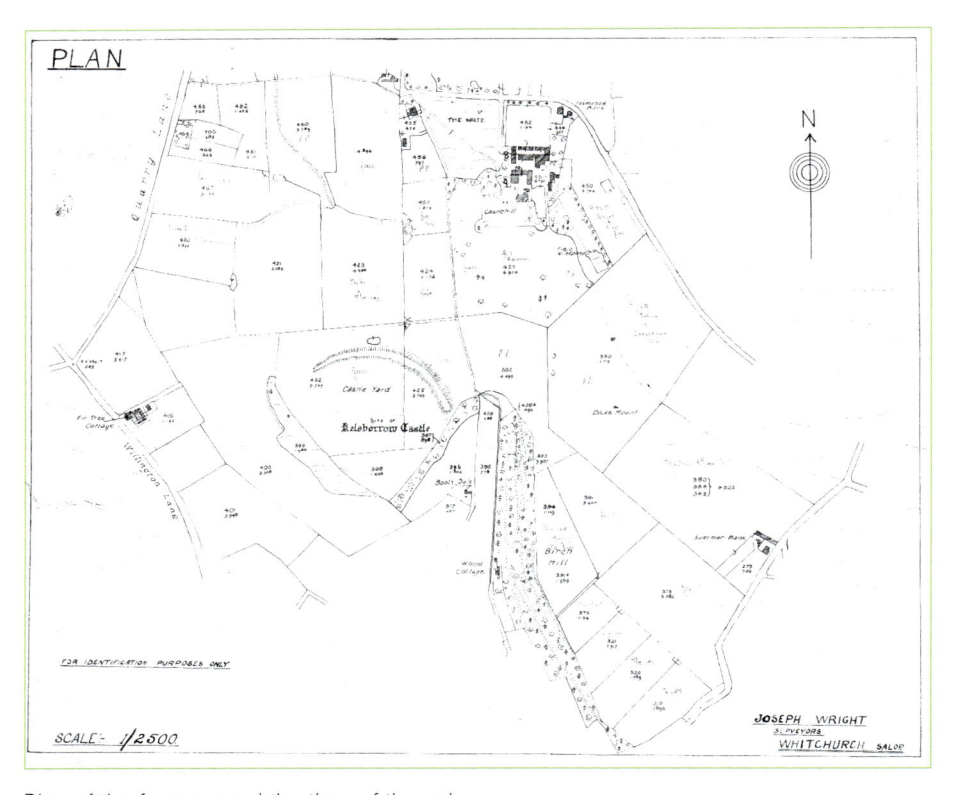

Plan of the farm around the time of the sale

It can be seen that the estate was extensive and had a number of sitting tenants. Mike's paternal grandfather, Donald Hardy bought the farm in 1933. He was a stockbroker originally from Derbyshire but living in Wilmslow, Manchester at the time of the sale. He and his New Zealand born wife, Elizabeth (Bessie) said that one of the reasons for the purchase was that their son John, born in 1928, suffered from tuberculosis (TB) and the move to the countryside would benefit him. This seems to be true as John thrived, together with his sister Joan, on the farm. John married Jill in 1952 and they raised a family of three sons and two daughters who all remain in the neighbourhood. They set up their home in Summer Bank, just a few fields away from Castle Hill, and Jill has remained in the family home to date.

The Castle Hill residence was extensively altered in 1934 and one quotation for the work was for a cost of £2500, equivalent to about £100,000 in today's monetary value.

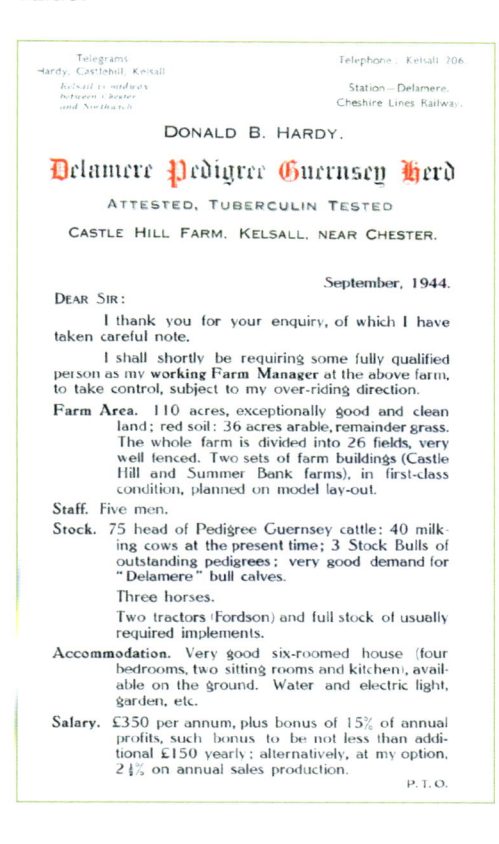

> Telegrams:
> Hardy, Castlehill, Kelsall
> *kelsall is midway
> between Chester
> and Northwich*
>
> Telephone: Kelsall 206
> Station – Delamere
> Cheshire Lines Railway
>
> **DONALD B. HARDY.**
>
> **Delamere Pedigree Guernsey Herd**
>
> ATTESTED, TUBERCULIN TESTED
>
> CASTLE HILL FARM, KELSALL, NEAR CHESTER.
>
> September, 1944.
>
> DEAR SIR:
>
> I thank you for your enquiry, of which I have taken careful note.
>
> I shall shortly be requiring some fully qualified person as my working Farm Manager at the above farm, to take control, subject to my over-riding direction.
>
> **Farm Area.** 110 acres, exceptionally good and clean land; red soil: 36 acres arable, remainder grass. The whole farm is divided into 26 fields, very well fenced. Two sets of farm buildings (Castle Hill and Summer Bank farms), in first-class condition, planned on model lay-out.
>
> **Staff.** Five men.
>
> **Stock.** 75 head of Pedigree Guernsey cattle: 40 milking cows at the present time; 3 Stock Bulls of outstanding pedigrees; very good demand for "Delamere" bull calves.
>
> Three horses.
>
> Two tractors (Fordson) and full stock of usually required implements.
>
> **Accommodation.** Very good six-roomed house (four bedrooms, two sitting rooms and kitchen), available on the ground. Water and electric light, garden, etc.
>
> **Salary.** £350 per annum, plus bonus of 15% of annual profits, such bonus to be not less than additional £150 yearly; alternatively, at my option, 2¼% on annual sales production.
>
> P.T.O.
>
> If you are interested in the appointment of which particulars are given on the other side of this sheet I shall be pleased to have very full details as to age, farming experience, family.
>
> Beyond general supervision the post also entails working for and on the land to obtain the best possible results and general upkeep in first-class order, and the situation is certainly "not one for the armchair critic."
>
> I shall be glad of your observations and be pleased to supply further details as requested.
>
> Interview arranged by appointment only; and no telegrams, please.
>
> The engagement will be the subject of a formal agreement.
>
> Yours truly,
>
> *Donald B. Hardy.*
>
> Submit copies (not originals) of any references you may think useful at this stage.
>
> P.S.—At the present time sales production is about £6,000 per annum. "Raising" once grown seed potatoes forms a valuable portion of this farm's produce; applicant should have a fair knowledge of potato growing.

Donald Hardy continued as a stockbroker and the farm was run by a farm manager and staff. He set up a pedigree herd of Guernsey cows producing tuberculin-free milk. A letter seeking a suitable candidate in 1944 gives an insight into the requirements and remuneration for the position.

Donald had set out to produce a very high quality product and this has been described in an article in The Chronicle, Saturday 5th June 1937, 'Tour of leading Cheshire Farms – Stockbroker sets out to fight TB - Mr Donald B Hardy's grand herd of Guernsey's.' .

Tuberculosis infected milk was a serious problem and around 1500 deaths occurred each year from TB of bovine origin. In 1937, Parliament promoted a scheme, known as the Attested Herds Scheme, whereby producers were given financial help in the form of a bonus to maintain herds free from tuberculosis. Such schemes, together with the pasteurisation of milk, at one time nearly eliminated the disease but it is interesting to note that TB can still be a problem in dairy herds

Captured Memories across the Hillforts of Cheshire - Kelsborrow

Part of the Guernsey Pedigree Herd in the 1940s – John Hardy is on the left and Joan Hardy is third from left.

today. Many cases have been attributed to infections coming from badgers although some would dispute this.

Donald Hardy was at the forefront of the push to produce TB free milk and he relied on maintaining a herd of pedigree Guernsey cattle and scrupulous attention to hygienic methods of milking, packaging and selling non-heat treated milk. In 1939, only about 3% of the dairy herds in England and Wales were attested. Castle Hill Farm's Guernsey herd was said to be one of the finest in the country. The herd numbered about 22 milking cows in 1937, each yielding around 3 gallons of milk per day which was considered to be extremely good. Donald travelled to Guernsey to obtain suitable stock of animals to increase the herd. The milk was sold in Perga containers (waxed cartons) so that milk bottles did not have to be returned and cleaned. The milk was kept cool at all times. These were significant improvements to normal production methods at the time. The milk was retailed locally as well as in Manchester and Liverpool. Castle Hill Farm was an early adopter of the vacuum method of milking.

Dairyman with vacuum milking equipment

68

During the war, evacuees from Liverpool were housed on the farm and Mike's grandmother Elizabeth helped to organise the evacuees around the area. There was some wartime activity on the hill. The Kelsall Home Guard was commanded by Captain Strong supported by Sergeant Major Flood and Sergeant Ellis Morrey. The vicar, Alan Roscamp taught the men semaphore on Kelsborrow Hill. In the later years of the war, prisoners-of-war were regularly seen on local farms and working in the forest. The so-called 'German Wall' on the road to Willington at Roughlow was built by prisoners-of-war.

"The van that brings you this BETTER Milk, Cream and HEALTH."

Donald Hardy died when John was about 19 and the farm passed to him in about 1947. John Hardy followed his father as a stockbroker, commuting from Delamere Station. He also diversified into managing a publicly owned sweet and confectionery business in Stockport but he always took a keen interest in the farm.

The farm was badly hit by the foot-and-mouth outbreak in 1968 and the pedigree herd was lost and not replaced. There is a large burial pit for the cattle on the farm. When the farm was re-stocked it was with a mixture of Guernsey and Friesian cows.

John Hardy sold off some of the paddocks over the years and the Castle Hill House was sold in 1987. Mike Hardy was the first to farm full time and the house he and his wife now occupy was built in 1991. Mike invested heavily in a new milking parlour and milk storage tanks but the milk industry has had some tough times through the introduction of milk quotas in 1983 and the low price for milk. The buildings were alright for their original use but it was difficult to adapt them for modern farming methods. He sold the dairy herd in 2003 and now concentrates on rearing dairy replacement cattle using organic production systems.

Castle Hill Farm has been described as a stunning film setting and the area has already featured in a popular TV drama, The Forsyte Saga.

Kelsall Transmitter Tower.

Above the farm are two masts. One is a large wooden structure operated for the control of civil aviation, military and Manchester airport. At one time it was permanently manned but nowadays much of the time it is remotely accessed by computer links. The mast is operated by National Air Traffic Services (NATS) and is the Kelsall Tx, Comms Station. NATS provides air traffic control services to aircraft flying in UK airspace, and over the eastern part of the North Atlantic. Last year, NATS handled some 2.1 million flights carrying around 200 million passengers. Safety is NATS' first and foremost priority in an efficient and cost-effective way

The history of the Kelsall site, known as Dick's Mount, stems from the formation of the Civil Aviation Authority in 1972. Although the site existed before that date as an aviation radio station belonging to the then Ministry of Aviation, it is likely to date from the 1950s and not to have been in existence during the Second World War.

During the 1950s the fledgling civil aviation industry required better infrastructure on the ground. The development of radio communications equipment, alongside that of ground based navigational aids providing guidance and assistance to aircraft required a number of sites throughout the UK to be acquired. It is likely that the site at Kelsall was obtained at this time. The early radio station may have consisted of a Nissan hut and a wooden mast of unknown type. During the early 1970s the current building at the site was constructed and the tower replaced with the one you see today.

The current tower at Kelsall is that of a Ministry of Defence design adopted and used by the Civil Aviation Authority, and is known as a standard Mk IV timber tower. The tower stands some 39 metres in height (120 feet) and is made from treated Douglas Fir.

Originally the tower would have only supported UHF and VHF aerials for communication with aircraft. The same style and type of aerials are still in service today. Over time, and to support the integrity of services, microwave links have been added to improve service reliability by adding additional routeing of circuits to and from the site. In addition to NATS services recent years have seen other service providers share our facilities providing mobile phone access points, pager systems, support services to the emergency services and more.

The site is one of many throughout the UK providing radio coverage for the safe routeing of all aircraft flying in UK airspace and will remain so for the foreseeable future. The fact is that if you have flown commercially from Manchester, Blackpool or Liverpool airports the pilot would be communicating with the air traffic controllers via Kelsall through the aerials supported by this Tower.

The other tower was erected more recently for Orange mobile telephone use.

Local Memories

Mike Hardy's sister, Sue Hardy told us of some of her thoughts about the hillside. "I have a very strong and passionate feel for the Boothsdale Valley (the name of which derives from the 'Valley at the herdsmen's shelters') and 'Little Switzerland' as we have always called the band of woodland that forms the perimeter to the family farm. I was born in the house in which my mother still lives and as a child and adult wandered across the fields with almost daily frequency. I recall looking down to what is now my cottage when a child and my father musing that he would be very happy if I wanted to live there one day. Shame he died before I did so. All the fields on the farm have names by which they are known and identified. As I sit in my office I can see the wall that is being rebuilt along the footpath under the trees. It is so good. I am almost in tears at the way it has restored the natural look and this will be enhanced as various green growth comes back along the top and bottom of the wall. Lovely to see the brambles etc cleared out from the 'no man's land' at the top edge of the field. Previous owners put the fence at a distance from the wall so that walkers did not touch their horses! I have fond memories of Mary Whalley who used to work on the farm bottling the milk and taught me as a very young child, how to milk a cow by hand! Someone I have known literally all my life."

Mary Whalley lived at Boothsdale Farm and she told us of some of the family history. Her parents bought the farm and 4-5 acres of fields in 1912 for £250 and she was born there in 1931 and lived at the property until about 1990. She had a hard life as her father died when she was 12 years old. The family kept a few animals but her father also worked for the Kenworthy estate breaking in the stud horses alongside Tommy Meakin who was responsible for training the horses. She said her brother had to mow their grassland with a scythe because of the steepness of the fields. She had to milk the cows her family had before she went to school. When she was 14 she started working for the Hardy family. Initially she worked in the house but later was responsible for the bottling of the milk. She remembers this was originally in waxed cartons but later they used glass bottles. Obviously she always walked up to Castle Hill Farm from Boothsdale and Sue can picture her emerging from the woods in her Wellington boots. Mary said her objective was to get up the steep hill each day without stopping. She told us that her brother had been the landlord of the Boot Inn at one time. Mary is now nearly 80 and still works several days a week at a local hotel.

Boothsdale (Little Switzerland) 1991

The Boot Inn lies at the foot of Boothsdale and was previously known as The Cat. It started in a dwelling in a row of cottages in the early 19th century. It would have been a simple wayside beer house and maybe of dubious reputation. It is perhaps a little strange that it was not situated on a main highway. Nowadays it has a fine reputation for good food and beer.

Nearby, Pearl Hole and Roughlow Farm are marked on the map. These names are derived from 'Spring Hollow' and 'Rough Mound' respectively.

Riddles in the Cliffs

On the western flank of Kelsborrow Castle the sandstone cliffs have been quarried for building stone on a relatively small scale and ad hoc basis. The actual date for the stone quarrying is unrecorded but the 19th century census returns for Delamere parish attest to the presence of several stone masons in the area. Several odd features have subsequently appeared in the cliffs which include carved and laid stone steps and a pair of stone gate posts; however, the most intriguing feature is a set of four seats carved in to an overhang in the cliff. At first glance these seats appear to have been slowly covered by decades of graffiti laid down by numerous ramblers and more local visitors to the cliffs including 'S KERR JUNE 1915' and 'E PUGH 20.6.58'. Closer inspection reveals that the seats are actually arranged as two pairs with a slight gap between the second and third seats above which is a deeply inscribed and neatly executed date of 1842. Furthermore, to the left and right of the date are four pairs of similarly deeply inscribed and well executed initials that also sit neatly above each of the four seats. The initials are arranged as follows:

The four seats carved in to the Kelsborrow cliffs in 1842

First seat – G W; Second seat – J A; Third seat – J R; Fourth seat – C C

These seats are hard to place in a context as they clearly pre-date the developments at 'Castle Hill' associated with the Halls and the Kenworthys, but they are at the same time the result of a lot of work by a skilled stone mason. As the initials are all different it suggests that the 'owners' of the 4 seats were not related, although the pairings of the seats might perhaps suggest two courting couples? On the other hand it may be no coincidence that the view from the seats would have over looked the lower lying Delamere Chapel (erected in 1817) and the date of 1842 may commemorate a significant event that is now forgotten.

There are other carved seats adjacent to the folly 'stand' on Birch Hill.

Willington Fruit Farm

Willington Fruit Farm Shop is in Chapel Lane, Willington and is run as a family partnership by the Winsor's. Ella Wood (nee Winsor) filled us in on some of the history of the farm.

Phil Winsor was West Country born and worked for Shell at Capenhurst but decided to move into farming in 1950 when he bought Hillside Farm. In 1958, the business expanded and Fir Tree Farm was bought from the Formston family who were dairy farmers. It is on this land that the stone carved seats can be found and the farm abuts the hillfort.

The Winsor Children Playing in a Shire Horse Box on Castle Hill Farm in the late 1950s

The first crops grown were strawberries, gooseberries, rhubarb and blackcurrants. In 1953 they planted the first apple orchard and some of these trees are still producing an abundance of fruit year after year even though they are well over 50 years old. Since then they have added raspberries, runner-beans, cabbage and much more seasonal produce as well as producing apple juice and cider. The Leylandii that now surround Fir Tree Farm were planted in 1971 by Phil Winsor with the help of a New Zealand worker employed on the farm. They are now of a considerable size and a start has been made to remove some of them, particularly on the hillfort ramparts. They are being replanted with broadleaf trees although the original area would have been meadowland in living memory.

References

1. 'Kelsall and Willington- A Personal Collection' Harold Hockenhull, C.C. Publishing, Chester, 2006. ISBN 0 949001 33 3
2. 'The Story of Kelsall' Elspeth Thomas, Masons Design and Print, Chester
3. 'Tour of leading Cheshire Farms – Stockbroker sets out to fight TB - Mr Donald B Hardy's grand herd of Guernsey's.' The Chronicle, Saturday 5th June 1937.

Captured Memories across the Hillforts of Cheshire - Kelsborrow

Captured Memories across the Hillforts of Cheshire

Artist's impression of Beeston Castle by Dai Owen

Beeston Castle, 2010

LIDAR view of Beeston Castle – see page xi

BEESTON CASTLE

77

Beeston

Beeston Crags

The appearance of Beeston Crags has changed dramatically over the years and the current, mainly wooded hilltop, would have been unrecognisable 60 years ago. Up to that time the land was grazed which would have controlled the growth of young trees and scrub. The site is still owned by the Tollemache estates. The estate was bought by John, 1st Lord Tollemache (1805-1890) member of Parliament for South Cheshire and later West Cheshire in 1840 who planted the pine trees to 'improve' the appearance of the castle and to 'frame' it from a distance and in particular his view from Peckforton Castle. He also terraced the outer bailey of the castle to enable marquees to be erected for fetes. He had the first gatehouse built in 1846 and this was extended in 1979. Peckforton Castle was built between 1844 and 1852.

An aerial photographs taken on 17th January 1947 by the RAF shows the castle to be free from trees and shrubs on the south-west side and only wooded on the steep escarpment where the shadow of the hill clearly shows how dramatically the crag stands out from the surrounding landscape.

Another picture taken on 14th June 1968 shows the crag was still largely without tree and shrub cover. The current

Beeston and Peckforton Castles, 17th January 1947

78

Captured Memories across the Hillforts of Cheshire - Beeston

activities by English Heritage are returning the hillside to its former state and making it once more an eye-catching sight.

Visitors were allowed to visit the grounds from 1850 when deer, goats and kangaroos (probably red necked wallabies) were kept on the hill. Wallabies were a fashionable accessory for well-to-do estates. There was a colony of wallabies living wild on The Roaches on the western edge of the Peak District that had probably escaped from a collection held near Leek in Staffordshire. They are quite well adapted to life in the UK but some say that they may have died out through a combination of cold winters and inbreeding. However, we have had reports that they are still present in the Roaches area.

Beeston Castle 14th June 1968

During the early 20th century the grounds were grazed by sheep which kept the bracken, invasive scrub and vigorous trees, such as silver birch and sycamore, in check. When ownership of the site was transferred to the Ministry of Works in 1959, the grazing stopped, allowing bracken and scrub to develop. This is somewhat ironic as bracken is very deep rooted (up to 2 metres) and can damage the underground archaeology we are trying to protect. A programme of landscape improvement began in around 2007 to eradicate the bracken and replanting of the 18th century hardwoods. The views as you approach, and from, the castle are much improved.

Captured Memories across the Hillforts of Cheshire - Beeston

Castle Entrance before the Bridge

Not all changes at the castle have met with approval. The Chester Chronicle of 16th February 1976 said that the new bridge to the castle was almost universally disliked shortly before it was finished. It was noted that it was not possible to construct the same type of bridge as existed in medieval times so it was decided to use a contemporary design. The bridge is now considered to have architectural merit in its own right.

The views from the castle are magnificent – eastwards to Jodrell Bank and beyond, to the chimneys of the power station at Conner's Quay, and the cathedrals and the Liver Building in Liverpool, southwards to the Long Mynd and across to the Clwydian Hills.

At the base of the mount are the caves. These were dug in the late 1700s to mid 1800s for sand extraction to be used in building and 'scouring' the bottoms of narrow boats.

Construction of the bridge

Adjacent to the Visitors' Centre there were stone masons huts from the late 1960s to the early 1990s used by the stone masons belonging to the Ministry of Works who had this as their base for the whole of the north-west region. The huts have now been demolished.

The completed Bridge

Archaeological Excavations

The monument (Beeston Castle) was placed in the guardianship of the Ministry of Public Buildings and Works in 1959. The subsequent campaign of consolidation and preparation for public display gave rise to successive campaigns of archaeological excavation. The excavation work was seasonal.

1968-73

These excavations were directed by Laurence Keen and were intended principally to clear modern material from the monument and display more of the medieval structure. In the inner ward it was hoped that excavation might reveal a greater surviving height of medieval walls, increasing safety to the visitor, who was at the time prohibited access. To begin with labour for most of the work was provided by the castle's 'direct labour team' and by H M Borstal and a local prison with archaeological supervision. Only during 1972-3 was a full archaeological team engaged aided by volunteers. Large quantities of spoil were removed from the inner ward which had accumulated during excavations of the well in 1842 and again in 1935. Some small scale work was undertaken on the inner ditch in 1972 whilst in the outer ward two of the towers at the outer gateway were partly excavated in 1973.

1975-85

Excavations were directed by Peter Hough using a large excavation team including many volunteers. Mechanical clearance of the inner ditch was preceded by further archaeological work in 1975-6 under the direction of Peter Hough. Subsequently, further excavations at the outer gateway took place prior to the construction of new access routes to the castle. Excavation in the outer ward commenced in 1980 following the discovery (as a surface find) of a Bronze Age palstave (a type of axe).

Beeston Castle dig 1981 – trench in outer bailey.

Captured Memories across the Hillforts of Cheshire - Beeston

These excavations helped to breed an entire generation of archaeologists in the Northwest some of whom are still practising including: Jill Collens and Alison Heke (Cheshire West and Cheshire Council), Ian Smith (Liverpool John Moore's University) Mark Fletcher (Matrix Archaeology) and Duncan Brown (Southampton City Council).

Tea break during the 1981 dig – Alison Heke (nee Jones) and Robin Brown

Motorcycle Hill Climbs

Hill climbs at Beeston Castle were organised by Nantwich Motorcycle Club and it was one of the biggest attractions of the post war years. The competition drew riders from around the country and was a tough one!

A section of bracken was cut away up the side of the hill and motorcyclists would have to make their way, without stopping, to the top of the course. The rider was not allowed to touch the floor with his feet once he had set off. If he did, that was his distance. A scramble to the top of the course finished the race. The one who got the furthest was declared the winner!

The Hill Climb, as remembered by Hector Wood.
"The hill climb took place on the Castle Side Farm side of the hill (being the steepest at about a 1 in 3 gradient). It created great interest over the years, but it was very hard work to get the track prepared each year. Labour for this was provided by local farmers such as Edgar Wood of Beeston Hall, Charles Ryder of Castle Gates Farm, Herbert Major and Leslie Winward of Castle Side Farm. Preparation involved scything the race track and then roping it off. This took most of the day. Spectators lined the track on each side and in dry weather, were showered with dust brought up by flying rear wheels of the bikes trying to reach the top. Very few did as I remember. Only one bike at a time made the attempt. At the end of the day, you can imagine the chaos at the gate with literally hundreds of people and bikes trying to get home."

One, rather painful, story linked to the hill climbs is the year that demolition expert Derek "Blaster" Bates secured some home made rockets to his motorbike to improve his chances of winning. Blaster enjoyed scrambling, hill climbing and stunt events, His most famous antic took place at Beeston Castle on 7th August 1952 on an early Norton. The rockets used a mixture of sodium nitrate and sugar. Off up the hill he went, unfortunately he was 12 feet in front of the bike. He ended up with burns on his legs and part of the rocket stuck in his back-side. Blaster asked the doctor if he would need stitches and was told. "Stitches?? We'll have to bloody darn". 72 hours later he was out of hospital on crutches but had to attend outpatients for a further 10 months. When his mate Walter took him home his wife Maud was there and said something along the lines "Oh, dump him in the corner, he'll be all right". A film of this rocket powered attempt is at www.blasterbates.info/timeline.

Derek Macintosh Bates stood 6ft 4in tall and bore a striking resemblance to John Wayne. He was born in Crewe on February 5, 1923 and died in Sandbach on September 1, 2006. He was an explosive and demolition expert and raconteur and much in demand as an after-dinner speaker. He spoke with a strong Cheshire accent. His tales feature coarse language and their content is equally strong stuff. On leaving the RAF, Bates started his own demolition business in Cheshire and soon became recognized as a leading exponent of high-stack chimney demolition, pioneering the way in which such buildings were demolished. He changed the landscape of northern England by single-handedly blowing up 54 chimney stacks at St Helens alone, earning the nickname "Blaster". In the early 1950s, as his reputation as a demolition expert spread both in Britain and abroad, Bates prepared the site of the Oulton Park racing circuit in Cheshire, which later furnished the setting for one his most hilarious and unrepeatable stories, "The Naming Of Knicker Brook", in which a semi-naked courting couple flee in disarray from one of his explosions.

The Treasure Seekers

Richard II stayed at Beeston Castle in 1399 before sailing from Chester to Ireland to quell a rebellion there. He was taken prisoner on his return by Henry Bolingbroke, Duke of Lancaster who became Henry IV. Richard's treasure was seized but legend has it that some was hidden away in the castle before he went to Ireland. It has never been found. There have been estimates that it could be valued at £200 million at today's prices.

There have been many searches since then and most have focussed on the well which sinks 124 metres (370 feet) to the level of the Beeston Brook. The first 192 feet of the shaft is about 6 feet wide is lined with masonry but below this it is carved in the natural rock.

Captured Memories across the Hillforts of Cheshire - Beeston

The book 'Picturesque Cheshire' by T A Coward in 1903 says that "long ago a man went down the well but came up lacking both treasure and the power of speech; he has never been able to reveal the horrors of the well". One report says that the well was cleared to the bottom in 1842.

Despite this, it has not deterred others from searching the well. The Daily Mail of 4th February 1935 reported an expedition by chemists and engineers from Northwich. They explored the well and three tunnels they discovered which lead off from the well. Such tunnels are not uncommon and are often known as Sally Ports. They are secret tunnels used as exits from the castle in the event of a siege, so the castle could be resupplied. One tunnel, at about 80 feet down, was said to go to Beeston Hall about 2 miles away. Beeston Hall itself was later burnt down by Prince Rupert so it could not be used by the Roundheads during the battles between the Roundheads and Royalists. Prince Rupert did avail himself of the hospitality of the hall and dined with the Lady before burning it down!

The Staffordshire press of 3rd November 1973 reported an investigation led by a consortium of 17 businessmen but there was no report of the treasure being found.

In 1976 the Chester Chronicle reported another expedition (23rd January 1976) by the White Hart Exploration Society of Bristol. They said their intention was purely archaeological and was not for the treasure. The presence of the side tunnels was confirmed.

The well at Beeston Castle, 1976

A camera was lowered down the well in April 2009 but it was found to be blocked at about 85 metres down. So, who knows, the treasure may still be there for the finding or perhaps a very happy Henry Bolingbroke was laughing all the way to his coffers a long time ago.

'Operation Dodo'

The peregrine falcon is a fairly rare sight in the UK so it is a delight to say that the species has bred successfully at Beeston for many years but not without the help of local residents.

Captured Memories across the Hillforts of Cheshire - Beeston

The peregrine *(Falco peregrins)* occurs as a resident bird of prey on all continents and is probably the most widely distributed of all birds. It is a matchless flyer and its stoop when chasing prey has been estimated at in excess of 240 kilometres per hour (150 miles/hour). The peregrine was the bird of choice for falconry in the past but during the late 19th century it was persecuted on the grouse moors of the UK. One of its favourite foods is pigeon, so during the Second World War its numbers were halved to protect the carrier pigeons so vital to the war effort. The population had started to recover but was badly hit by poisoning from the use of organochlorine pesticides during the 1950s – 1960s so by 1967 the population was at a seriously low ebb.

Peregrine

The peregrine had been nesting at Beeston for a number of years prior to 1993 but in the previous 5 years poachers had attacked the nests and stolen the eggs or young chicks. Cheshire Police launched 'Operation Dodo' in 1993 with the help of 85 local volunteers to watch over and protect the falcons at Beeston Crag. That year PC Mike Wellman, Cheshire Police, Wildlife and Environmental Officer, reported that all 4 eggs had hatched and fledged successfully. The bird surveillance not only resulted in the nests being protected but the neighbourhood watch had a knock on effect so that 3 people were charged with burglary, 4 with public order offences, one for possessing an offensive weapon and recovered 2 stolen vehicles. Who ever thought that crime was restricted to big cities. It just goes to show that communities pulling together can achieve remarkable results.

Janet Blinkhorn had watched the cliffs from Home Farm below the crag but there had been no further problems until 2008 which prompted the watch to be re-established. Three peregrine chicks were stolen on 20th May 2008 by 6 men who were seen with ropes and rucksacks and probably abseiled down the crag. The birds were all grown and it is likely they were taken for use in falconry. At the time they could have been worth about £700 each.

The 70-strong volunteer Beeston Peregrine Watch was set up in 2009 had kept a look-out on the nest on the crag, day and night, between April and June. Bernhard Wright from the Watch and Broxton Barn Owl Group said: "The end result was three juvenile flyers around the crag at Beeston and people can take great pride". The chicks were successfully ringed when Dave Bradley abseiled down the cliff, collected the birds for ringing and DNA testing before returning them to their parent. The DNA testing allows stolen birds to be traced and identified.

Village Fetes

The tradition of village fetes at Beeston Castle was started by Lord Tollemarche from as early as 1851 and the fetes were always held around the 23-24 June just after the summer solstice. They continued until 1909. In 1851 the fete was in aid of the widows and orphans of the Peckforton District of the Independent Order of Oddfellows and was said to have been visited by 2500 people and raised about £200 (equivalent to £11,000 in 2010).

The fete moved to August Monday in 1945 after the war and was in aid of the church. The 1946 fete raised £400 and it was in 1948 that the fete was linked with the motorcycle, hill climbing test. The history of the 'Beeston Castle Fete' has been documented in a book produced by Bunbury residents in 1996.

The value of a village fete is well summarised in the minutes of the fete organisers in1981. "The purpose is fourfold. It is vital for St Boniface church to meet the daily running expenses; the better to get to know each other; it is great fun (weather permitting) and it is great public relations and hospitality for Bunbury." These objectives could be applied to many other local, rural events and which are often in decline in this day and age.

Entertainment and Historical re-enactments

Beeston has frequently been used as the backdrop for a variety of historical re-enactments as part of a programme of bringing history to life. Just a few are:

- Mustering for the King in July 1992
- Civil war re-enactment in May 1975 by the national societies of the King's Armies and The Roundhead Association
- Medieval re-enactments in 1998, July 2000 and May 2006 by Harlech Medieval Society
- Roman fun and games in July 2007
- Napoleonic wars recreated by Wellington Redcoats
- Medieval mayhem in July 2009

The arts have not been neglected either. Visiting players have presented many notable productions including:

- Walkabout presentation of Shakespeare's Macbeth by the Midsommer Actors.
- Romeo and Juliet presented in 2000 by the Chapterhouse Theatre Company
- Inner State Theatre Company's presentation of Hoodwinked in July 2000 about Robin Hood and Maid Marion
- Perrotts Puppet Players presented 'Garwaine and the Green Knight' in August 2007, about Garwaine's journey from King Arthur's Camelot to Hautdesert which may well have been a reference to Beeston Castle.
- Simon Cobbold created mixed media sculptures as part of English Heritage's year of public sculpture in 2000.

Darker Moments

On 27th October 1913, the Peckforton Hills were battered by a freak 'cyclone' and hundreds of trees were uprooted and cattle killed.

Beeston Castle in the winter of 1963 was bleak. It was one of the severest winters experienced with extensive snow coverage all around. Even the River Dee froze over allowing people to take an afternoon stroll on the river.

The view from the top of Beeston Crags in 1967 was a sad one indeed. In October of that year the first case of foot and mouth disease was confirmed in Cheshire. Foot and mouth is a highly contagious viral disease which affects cattle pigs and sheep. Cases continued to rise until February 1968. Mass burials and pyres of destroyed cattle and pigs would have been seen, scattered across the countryside. Not only was the loss of stock devastating to the rural community but there were considerable fears about the future of farm workers' jobs. January 1968 was also the time when severe snow falls had gripped Cheshire and the A41 from Bulkeley to Peckforton was completely blocked. Cheshire and Shropshire were the worst affected counties for this foot and mouth outbreak. In December 1967 there were 1000 cases in Cheshire with well over 125,000 animals being slaughtered with more to follow.

The disease returned to the UK in 2001 with Cumbria being the worst affected area. Another outbreak was confined to the Home Counties in 2007. Whilst, fortunately, these outbreaks did not directly affect Cheshire too badly, they did cause considerable disruption to stock movements and rural life. Beeston Castle was closed as a precaution during the 2001 outbreak.

Climbing

Beeston Castle is a fine looking sandstone outcrop. Many people have climbed routes here in the past. The black walls and overhangs below the castle are bigger than anything else in Cheshire. However the land is looked after by the Department of the Environment who in their infinite wisdom have decided that climbing is forbidden.

References:

1. 'Beeston Castle', Robert Liddiard and Rachel McGuicken, English Heritage, 2007, ISBN 978 1 85074 925 7
2. Arial photographs: English Heritage, National Monuments Record public archive.
3. Reference: Ellis P (ed), 1993. Beeston Castle, Cheshire: Excavations by Laurence Keen & Peter Hough, 1968-85. English Heritage Archaeological Report No 23. pp 10 & 15-16.
4. Hill climbs: www.blasterbates.info/timeline.
5. Treasure: 'Picturesque Cheshire' by T A Coward, 1903
6. Treasure: The Daily Mail of 4th February 1935
7. Treasure: Staffordshire press of 3rd November 1973
8. Treasure: Chester Chronicle, 23rd January 1976
9. Peregrines: 'Fauna Britannica' , Stefan Buczacki. Published by Hamlyn, 2002. ISBN 0600 613925
10. Peregrines: Daily Mail, 16th July 1993; Daily Express 16th July 1993.
11. Peregrines: Chester Chronicle 27th June 2008
12. Peregrines: Chester Chronicle 10th September 2009;
13. Peregrines: Chronicle Extra 15th June 2009
14. Climbing: Sandstone Climbing in Cheshire and Merseyside by Alan Cameron-Duff and Peter Chadwick. 1998 Published by Stone Publishing and Design, Waterfoot, Rossendale, Lancashire BB4 9AG

Captured Memories across the Hillforts of Cheshire

MAIDEN CASTLE

Artist's impression of Maiden Castle by Dai Owen

Bickerton, 2010

LIDAR view of Maiden Castle – see page xi

89

Maiden Castle

In the 19th Century, George Ormerod described "the precipitous elevations of the Bickerton Hills, whose bare and abrupt crags crowned with the earthworks of a British Fortress ……. The eye commands the long line of the broken terminations of this mountainous range, with minor well-wooded elevations scattered below." The view is very different nowadays as the slopes are clothed in woodland. However, the National Trust is returning an area around the hillfort to its previously heathland nature.

This picture, of an unknown date, is labelled 'Broxton Hills' as the whole ridge was at one time collectively known by this name but nowadays each hill has its own identity. The view is probably taken from near to Broxton village towards the ridge, with Raw Head in the centre.

Renewed Heathland

The heathland of the southerly hill went unmanaged from the 1940s until 1983, when 66 hectares (160 acres) of land were acquired by the National Trust; as a result of a bequest by Ian Dennis. The Trust's holding was extended by 51 hectares (130 acres) in 1991 after money was donated by Leslie Wheeldon. Much of the southerly hill and the western escarpment of the northerly hill were notified as two separate Sites of Special Scientific Interest in 1979.

Christopher Widger, National Trust Countryside Manager Cheshire and Wirral, explained the significance of the habitat around Maiden Castle.

"Many people will be aware, that Bickerton Hill is primarily significant for its high quality lowland heath and we are lucky to have in this wonderful site, on our doorstep, possibly the best example of this habitat in the whole of North-West England. Indeed, during the 1970s Bickerton Hill was designated a Site of Special Scientific Interest (SSSI) for its lowland heathland flora and fauna. But why is heathland so important?

Generally our heathland developed as the 'wildwood' was cleared in the later prehistoric and Roman periods and thus, for probably at least 2000 years, for countless generations of people, Bickerton and other nearby areas would have been known and valued as lowland heath. Characterised by its openness, and blend of heather, bilberry, gorse and soft grasses growing on impoverished soils, it was a resource for grazing and for the cutting of furze (gorse) and turf for fuel. It was not until grazing declined, due to economic reasons after the last war that encroaching scrub and birch began to change the scene.

So trees are a very recent phenomenon on the hill and they threaten the sustainability of the heath by shading out other vegetation, by providing an unwanted seed source and increasing the nutrient levels of the soil. The 1st edition OS map of 1882 (where individual trees were identified) shows virtually no trees - local residents remember cattle grazing as recently as the 1950s before the birch trees you see today seeded themselves. It could be said therefore, that lowland heath is a fundamental part of our national heritage and probably constitutes our earliest form of managed landscape.

The perceived value of heathland in terms of a resource, a habitat, landscape, and our heritage, is under threat. Statistically lowland heath is rarer and declining faster than rainforest, yet partly due to its profile, few would deny the importance of conserving the latter. Since the 1800s, 84% or our lowland heath has been lost. Of this loss, 40% has occurred in the last 50 years with the associated extinction of and threat to numerous rare, notable and endangered species of birds, reptiles, mammals and invertebrates including the adder, the common lizard, the Green Hairstreak butterfly and numerous other rare species of invertebrate. We are lucky to have the pied flycatcher, the little owl and crossbills amongst many other species of bird using the hill whilst it is here that the polecat was first recorded in Cheshire. Such species are just a small selection of those which, without such an environment, could be lost.

The loss of lowland heath, which will continue if we do not act. With a few renowned exceptions heathland is highly fragmented, the average patch in

England being less than 18 hectares (Ha). The ecological value of any habitat is directly proportional to scale, and thus it is important to consider scale and interconnection between similar areas, if optimum benefit is to be gained. Bickerton now has around 45 Ha of regenerating heathland and the interconnection of these areas has been a priority.

As a conservation organisation, the National Trust has a statutory duty to ensure that the SSSI at Bickerton is managed appropriately and that losses are stopped and trends reversed. Heathland is also a target habitat under Cheshire's Biodiversity Action Plan. After the Trust acquired the site during the 1980s, having allowed the then existing lease to the MOD to expire, it embarked upon a heathland restoration project. In partnership with Natural England, the Forestry Commission, the Cheshire Wildlife Trust and latterly, the Sandstone Ridge Econet Partnership (SREP) Project, the restoration continues to this day, with the invaluable support of diverse and numerous volunteers, who, in their spare time have actively contributed during the last 3 years alone, over 12,000 hours in supporting the management, restoration and protection of our local landscape. The objective has been to restore roughly half the site as Heathland, a target which has been met, whilst managing the remaining 45 Ha as woodland. So what does the future hold?

On the heath, we will concentrate on the promotion of re-establishment of heathland flora, for example, by using traditional grazing which had been in place for so long, until the latter half of the 20th century, which will ensure that the natural processes of regeneration of birch trees is suppressed. Encroaching bracken will be controlled and access will be ensured for walkers and horse riders alike.

Elsewhere, the development of areas designated as woodland will take precedence. These areas, including Hether Wood at the south-western end of the hill, which is designated as a Site of Biological Interest (SBI) are managed under the Forestry Commission's English Woodland Grant Scheme. This scheme is designed to aid and promote a mixed range of, predominantly native species, with a range of age structure and where a blend of ground flora, shrub layer and trees exist in harmony with one another, providing the greatest potential habitat for our wildlife. Selective removal of some non-native trees and trees which threaten to crowd or suppress potential veteran specimens are also removed. Some will be retained as dead wood for associated organisms such as fungi, mosses, lichens and specialist invertebrates."

Around the Hillfort

The WI Handbook of 1951 mentions that "the hills provided the silver sand used for scouring the dairy vessels, vats and cheese moulds...... An interesting local industry in bygone days was the making of 'besoms' for the cleaning of shippons, farmyards and dairy floors etc. The hills provided the materials for the making of besoms; heather and young birch were tightly bound together. Many people picked bilberries (whinberries) on the hills. Women and children could raise enough money to keep the families in clothes throughout the year, or keep them in food throughout the winter."

From the hillfort your eye is drawn to the village of Brown Knowl with its distinctive Methodist chapel. This was altered in 1913 to its present structure and in the grounds is the resting place of John Wedgwood (1788 - 1869) who was one of the leading figures in the Primitive Methodist movement. Further afield there are views of Fullers Moor to the north and the black and white building of Broxton Old Hall to the west.

The economy of this area was based on farming and the 1841 census for Broxton showed that of a population of 458 people there were 24 farmers and 80 more men employed to work on farms. The number of people employed in agriculture had already started to decline by 1901 and that trend has continued. The cessation of grazing on the hills is largely responsible for the loss of the heathland and the growth of trees covering the hills.

Mrs Rosemary Aspinall (nee Waterhouse) remembers times in the Maiden Castle area.

"On 15th April 1960 (when I was 11), I found a flint arrow-head on a sandy track on Bickerton Hill. I presented it to the Grosvenor Museum but asked for it back after a couple of years or so when it had still not been put on display. I have kept it safely ever since.

> The Journal of the Chester And North Wales Architectural Archaeological And Historic Society Volume 48 1961 described the flint arrow head from Bickerton Hill as: "A barbed and tanged flint arrow-head, of the usual Bronze Age type, found by Miss Rosemary Waterhouse while she was walking on the top of Bickerton Hill in April 1960 and subsequently presented to the Grosvenor Museum (11OP60). The approximate find-spot was about half a mile north-east of the Iron Age hill-fort known as Maiden Castle (Nat. Grid Ref. 503534 on sheet 109).

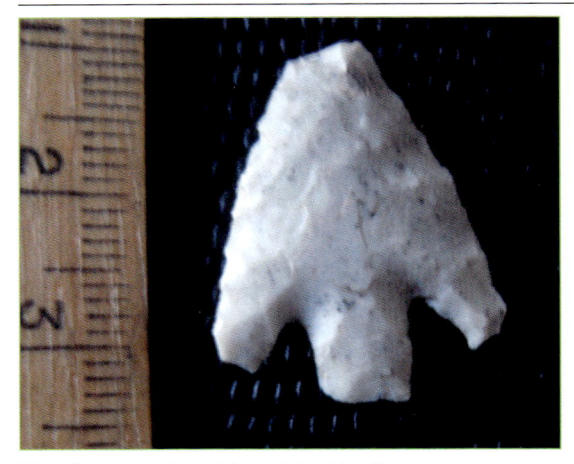

Captured Memories across the Hillforts of Cheshire - Maiden Castle

The flint arrow-head found by Mrs Rosemary Aspinall on Bickerton Hill in 1960

"When I was very young, petrol was rationed but we spent many happy days travelling from our home in Bromborough on the Wirral to Beeston and Bickerton Hill. Picking bilberries was a favourite activity.

From 1970 to 1981 I was personal assistant to Major Peter Moore, the Countryside Officer for Cheshire County Council. Later he was re-designated Director of the newly formed Countryside & Recreation Division. The Recreational Ways Officer was a very keen walker called Jack Baker and the Sandstone Trail was his brain-child and it was very interesting working on early projects such as this.

As a family we were always keen walkers and know this whole area well. Today my husband and I still enjoy walking the mid Cheshire paths and admiring the views from the sandstone ridge."

The Sandstone Trail long-distance footpath opened in 1974; it then started in Duckington, immediately south of the southerly hill. The Sandstone Trail Race was launched three years later. A total of 8500 walkers on the Sandstone Trail were recorded by the National Trust between January and March 2006, and the trust has estimated that 8000 dog walks occur annually within the Bickerton Hill SSSI. A 2008 proposal to construct a 60 metre wind-monitoring mast adjacent to Bickerton Hill met with local protest, and was rejected by Crewe and Nantwich Borough Council.

The Sandstone Trail

Quarrying took place at various sites on the hills, including Maiden Castle from the 17th century. Sandstone was extracted for building, and sand for use as a scouring agent. An iron rock-splitting wedge dating from the 17th century was found during excavations of Maiden Castle in 1996 as part of the battle clearances programme by the army.

Professor William J Varley undertook a programme of excavation at Maiden Castle in two successive seasons between 1934 and 1935 under the auspices of the 'Bickerton Camp Scheme'. William Varley was a Professor in the Department of Geography at the University of Liverpool and he had the idea of recruiting labour from the clubs for the unemployed being run by the Liverpool Occupational Centres Committee. Whilst other volunteers working on the Maiden Castle excavations included high school pupils and members of the Liverpool Rambler's Association.

The Sandstone Trail Race

The race, which is run under the Fell Runners Association (FRA) rules, follows part of a route developed from a favourite training run of Deeside Orienteering Club. The Sandstone Trail Race is held annually, in mid-autumn, and consists of two alternative races run concurrently, both following sections of the Sandstone Trail Path.

Since its inception in 1977 the race has attracted a regular following around Merseyside and the Welsh borders. Anyone running the 'A' race under two hours is likely to be a prize-winner, with good club runners finishing in around 2h 30m on a dry year. Beating one hour on the 'B' race was a worthwhile target up until 2006, but with the additional length that was added this may now be unachievable.

Numbers are limited to 190 for each race (previously 150) and these limits are often approached before the closing date. The race atmosphere is friendly and informal but organisation is tight, assisted by an army of volunteers, St John Ambulance and the co-operation of the Cheshire Police. On the day results are available, handsome trophies are presented under the massive beech trees in Delamere Forest, and runners and helpers alike still have time for a picnic in the forest or a lunchtime pint.

The 'A' Race is 27.5km (17.1 miles) with 655m climb starting from Duckington opposite the Iron Age hill fort of Maiden Castle and is ideal for the more experienced runner. For the first 7 miles the race follows the highest sections of the ridge, climbing to the trig point at Rawhead, 746ft, where the red chiselled cliffs resemble the Wild West more than Cheshire. The race has a total climb of 2150 feet (excluding the stiles!) made up of frequent short climbs.

Captured Memories across the Hillforts of Cheshire - Maiden Castle

The 'B' Race is 17.0km (10.6 miles) with 288m of climb starting from Beeston and is better suited for those wishing to try their hand at trail running. This race started in 1979 as a ladies race and, initially, only prizes in that category were awarded although men did compete. Now both races are open to men and women runners.

Both races finish in Delamere Forest where the prizes are presented. A 5 mile 'C' race lapsed in 1982.

A Quiet Place?

As well as being an exceptionally beautiful area, it is a vibrant place of work and recreation for many. Dave Morris has been the National Trust warden for Helsby Hill and Maiden Castle areas since February 1992 and was appointed when the NT acquired the second half of the hill. He knows every path, stile, fence and tree intimately and has been involved with the restoration work throughout his time there. He has made several appearances on TV to explain and promote the work of the Trust including being interviewed by Kate Simms for the BBC in August 2008 about the sweet chestnuts and the heathland restoration scheme.

He told me it is estimated that there were more than 8000 visitors to the area each year and the adventurer and explorer, Sir Ranulph Fiennes is a regular runner across the hills.

Dave works with a small team of volunteers from the Chester and Merseyside areas and other trainee wardens. The area is a workplace for many and he regularly hosts groups of people such as students from Reaseheath College studying heathland and woodland management as well as Probation Services from Liverpool and Crewe & Nantwich. Horse riding is allowed by permit from Dave and he even issue about 5 licences each year for model aircraft flying, not to mention the influx of people completing the Sandstone Trail run.

Captured Memories across the Hillforts of Cheshire - Maiden Castle

Military involvement

Cheshire was frequently crossed by enemy planes on their way to bombing missions in Liverpool and some incendiary bombs fell in the vicinity of the hills. Other targets included the Rolls Royce factory in Crewe. A whole line of bombs was dropped across Bickerton by the Italians and just missed the schoolhouse and the church. Prisoners of War were used as labourers at Pool Farm and elsewhere in the region.

Many men were excluded from the draft such was the need to keep them working on the land to produce essential food supplies. In 1940 the Home Guard 5th Cheshire (Broxton) Battalion was formed. They had a hut in one of the hollows in Maiden Castle and there was a nightly patrol mounted during 1940 and 1941. The hut was equipped with beds and two men patrolled whilst two slept.

In 1948 the Cheshire County Council fire Brigade was called out to control bracken fires on Bickerton Hill caused by army cadets using incendiary ammunition.

The area around Maiden Castle was used for military training exercises between 1939 and 1995. The army had a lease on half of the hill from Maiden Castle southwards. It was frequently used for training camps, night exercises and a 2-inch mortar range. Empty cases can still be found scattered over the hill. There was also a hand-grenade range near to the current car park. The area was covered in slit trenches and other army excavations. Towards the Brown Knoll end, in what is locally known as Cuckoo Rock Valley, there was an anti-tank range. Two steel posts about 30 feet high were erected about 200 yards apart. A steel cut-out of a tank was suspended from a steel rope

97

between the towers and slowly drawn down the valley so that army personnel could practice with ant-tank rifles with bullets being embedded in the slope below Maiden Castle.

The lease ended in 1995 and the army then undertook a clean-up operation over the next three years. Thousands of spent 2-inch mortar shells were removed together with Piatt rockets and other ordnance. Fortunately only about 6 live mortars were found and these were detonated in a controlled explosion on site. Although live ammunition was rare, visitors should treat any suspicious items with caution as there is no guarantee that all explosives have been found.

Kitty's Stone

Kitty's Stone is a 2-tonne block of sandstone with commemorative plaques placed in position in 1992. It is in memory of Kitty Wheeldon (nee Scott), the beloved wife of Leslie Wheeldon. Mr Wheeldon made a very generous donation which allowed the National Trust, with help from the Countryside Commission, to purchase Bickerton Hill from the Oulton Park Estates.

The original plan was for an obelisk to mark the spot but this was changed to the sandstone memorial which was prepared by a stone-mason from Nantwich. The stone was installed by Dave Morris and his team. The poems on the memorial are by Leslie Wheeldon (ALDW) and remember places which had particular significance to him and his wife. Two of them are reproduced here.

> As o'er the fells you walked with me
> In grey plaid skirt and coat of fawn
> So, heavenly father, she's clad for thee.
> Now o'er the fells she walks with thee.
>
> When up the Cerrig Llyn I gaze
> I'll think of you and other days
> Of rocks and stones and falls dull roarin'
> Of heathered fells and blood red rowan
> The stones I've seen with you my dear
> The distant views and waters clear
> All these I'll see and think them poorer
> Now that I lack you, my dear.

The cottage had 65 acres of land and George's Uncle Bill had been crippled from birth and couldn't walk until he had an operation at about 12 which allowed him to walk with the aid of a crutch. He kept 4 cows and a yearling and since there was no water on the hill these had to be taken down to be watered at the pond adjacent to Pool Farm each day. Butter from the milk was sold every Saturday at Malpas when they went by cart for shopping. Farming would not have provided a sufficient living for the family so he also worked as a roadsman, snared rabbits for sale in Brown Knoll and cobbled people's boots, shoes and clogs. The cottage had no electricity and even when a scheme was suggested in the late 1940s his great-aunt didn't want it as it was 'bad for the eyes'. She lived to the great age of 95.

The cottage was originally thatched, later covered by metal and then asbestos sheeting and this is probably why the house survived. Many other cottages on the hill were knocked down when they were empty. George was told that deer were kept on the hill in the 1920-30s by the Cholmondeley estate for hunting and grazing. Bilberry bushes covered the hillside and the kids were sent out with a jar each to collect the fruit to raise money for necessities such as clothing.

George visited his uncles very regularly on his bike and remembers it as a happy and exciting time. His Uncle Arthur was a timber feller and George helped him collect pea sticks, short birch twigs cut with a billhook, which were sold for 1/- a bundle off a horse and cart around the area. His uncle was very mechanical and one of the first people in the area to own a chain saw. He was adept at the use of 'black powder' for blowing up tree stumps and rock outcrops when called upon. His Uncle Harry was more domesticated and didn't socialise as much but he did have a Ford 8 car – licences weren't needed in those days. George's mother lived at Hampton when she was married and had been in service but the cottage was always George's second home. George was a welder and fabricator, and was self-employed for the last 15 years of his working life.

Between 1900 and 1924 Larkton Hill belonged to the Cholmondeley Estate before being sold to Arthur Shore and then in 1935 it was bought by the Dennis family. George says that many of the beech, Scots Pine and Larch trees were planted around 1937 by Mrs Dennis. Ian Dennis inherited the hill, including the cottage. He had lost both legs in a railway accident and spent many months living in a motor-home on the hill. George has fond memories of Ian Dennis. He was a great man for motor sports despite his injuries and converted his cars for hand operation. He encouraged the Nantwich Motorcycle Club to hold circuits and trials on the hill and the Landrover Club held weekend meets when as many as 100 cars would be there for hill climbing events. He had a very early interest in 16mm film making of the motor events on the hill and in the 1970s he toyed with video making despite the heavy and cumbersome equipment that was required in those days. He died aged about 64/65 and gifted the land to the National Trust.

George said the army made a considerable mess of the hills with dug-outs all over the place and he found many items left by the troops such as cigarette lighters and coins. Most of the trainees were Officer Cadets form Eaton Hall. During the exercises, flares were often tripped and went off like firework displays. They drifted down on parachutes which were collected and used as handkerchiefs. The bren gun carriers were small tanks on tracks which turned the land into mud baths but the tracks went right to the top of the hill so it was possible to drive up to Maiden Castle. He said that fires were frequent on the hill but the birches and heather re-grew.

Above all George spoke of the happy childhood he had spent on the hill and ever since; the beautiful surroundings, the birds and the quietness – marvellous!

Bob Bourne lived in Pool Farm all his life but unfortunately passed away about 3 years ago. His family bought the farm in about 1860-70 when they walked their cows from Congleton. There was no water on the farm until his grandfather built a dam and made the pool. The water also supplied Larkton Hall. Mains water did not arrive until 1937. There were many small wells and springs on the hill but these have now dried up.

The hillside was surrounded by small-holdings or squats of about 3 acres which had to have smoke coming from the chimney between dawn and dusk. There are nowhere near as many children now as there were in the past. He thinks there are about 6 now in the area compared to 18 when he was young. Many of the houses are now owned by commuters.

He remembers the army arriving in 1939 when the first to be trained were Czech but says that the military use can be traced back to the Boer War. He said the army burnt off the hilltop many times. During World War 2, the Pioneer Corps was stationed at Broxton Old Hall and the Home Guard had a shed on the hill for sleeping in. Three bombs fell in the neighbourhood and an enemy plane crashed and the 3 surviving crew members were captured.

He believed Mr Dennis had an alcohol problem which led to his railway accident in France. He died in the 1980s and his estate was left to three nephews. He said it was nice to see the hill going back to an open space. There had always been some bracken on the hill but it had spread. In his youth, the hill was a mass of heather and bilberry.

References:

1. Sand: WI Handbook of 1951
2. 'A Local History of Broxton, Duckington and Harthill.' Written and Researched by Wendy Bawn, Rebecca Dakin and Carol Shadbolt. Edited by Helen Bate (July 2004)
3. CDs of Interviews by Vanessa Nuttall, December 2003 held by the The National Trust, Cheshire Countryside Office, Macclesfield Road, Nether Alderley, Cheshire SK10 4UB.
4. Sandstone Trail Race: www.deeside-orienteering-club.org.uk/sstrail
5. 'Walking Cheshire's Sandstone Trail' Tony Bowerman. Northern Eye Books, 2008. ISBN -10: 0-9553557-1-0: ISBN-13: 978 -0 9553557-1-4.
6. 'Circular Walks along the Sandstone Trail' Carl Rogers. Mara Books, 5th Edition September 2009. ISBN 978-1-902512-10-5.

Final Thoughts

Captured Memories

Today
You and I, breathless, climb the steep to the Hill top.
Sturdy boots and trainers. The dog runs free
Along the skinny sandy tracks.
We see spread the fat Cheshire plain, embroidered with hedges.
We walk for the exercise. And the view.
The children play "Hide and Seek", and find a shaped stone.

Who formed it?

1970
Your father and mine, dirt-streaked, climb the cliff.
Overalls and rubber boots. The dog shivers.
They see that posy of hedges ring around
The bodies of cattle. A violent view
Of frozen rivers and smouldering death.
The death of farms.
The children play "Ring a Roses" and find a flint.

A hint of past handiwork?

1950
Your auntie and mine, giggling
Off the train and charabanc.
Sandals and nylons, with Ginger Beer and butties.
Climb the road to The Hill. A holiday
Hot day all day sunny, after
The Blackout of War. One long picnic.
The dog has a new red collar. And
The children play "Tick and ON" and drink lemonade.
Find a little broken pot.

Who drank out of this?

1940
Your grandmother and I stay home. Black windows
Winding wool and knitting squares. Blankets for the troops.
No Hill climbing. Black and OUT OF BOUNDS
To all except rough uniforms and leather boots.
Trenches cut and bunkers sunk
Through round stone walls long buried.
The dog dare not bark or whine.
And the children, quiet, make dolls from old socks,
Aeroplanes from bits of wood.

Who made those walls? Do we care?
We have a war to win.

1910
Our great- grandfathers, red in face,
Climb the Hill for bilberries to sell,
Or silver sand for scouring pots.
Smocks and slops, frayed hand-me downs.
Hot days, back-breaking work. No time to see the view.
The wench minds the cows, milks by hand.
The dog pulls at his chain, bares his teeth.
The children play "Piggy Back" and find an arrow head.

Who fired an arrow?

Before
Our fore-fathers climbed the Hill
Barefoot, rugged cloths and furs.
The dogs ran packed, obedient, fierce.
They saw a safety.
A view, protected by cliff and marsh.
Soft stone to hand-shape walls, Flint for tools.
Water clear and constant. Grass for cattle.
Trees for fire and fence.

They stopped. And shaped the land.

And the children played.

Barbara Foxwell

As a child, I might have thought that the history of England only started with the Romans; such was the teaching of the day. It is becoming increasingly clear that we had a long and sophisticated ancestry stretching far back beyond that. It is likely that there isn't a square metre of England that has not been touched by our predecessors in some way – the construction of a grand mansion, the ploughing of a field or a sapling trodden underfoot which never developed into a mighty oak. Our past shapes and influences us. We live in, and are a part of, our surroundings. It has even been calculated that each of us breathes in a considerable number of molecules from the air exhaled by Leonardo da Vinci or an iron-age farmer, or anybody else for that matter!

During the compilation of this book, I have been fascinated by the way seemingly ordinary areas of the county have had a profound effect. Take for example the small school at Delamere which became the model for school dinners throughout the country or the farm at Kelsborrow which led the way in the production of clean, uninfected milk. Although never used in anger, the bunker at Helsby was manned by well-meaning volunteers hoping to protect us from the perceived menace from the cold war. Future visitors may wonder why they can pick up spent mortar shells on a National Trust property on Bickerton Hill.

Although the Hillforts are important archaeological sites, they are also part of a living landscape. It is essential that present, and future generations, will be able to use and enjoy these prominent positions in many different ways. Nowadays, it is probably unthinkable to hold motorbike hill-climbs on the listed site at Beeston Castle but we should give careful consideration as to whether such high levels of protection will inhibit the enjoyment of our natural resources in other ways. Many people are reluctant to accept change but this book shows that our countryside is constantly changing. In my view, it is extremely risky to say we want to 'stop the clock' at any one point in our history. A treeless ridge may appeal to some whilst woodland is the choice of others. As with many things, balance and variety may be the best compromise.

It is human nature to try and order and understand our environment and it is the knowledge of small events that can add colour and interest to a country walk. We hope that this publication will stimulate others to increase this pool of knowledge. Many people think they have little to offer – one lady said to us "I'm not a true Helsby resident as I've only lived here 70 years!" Her memories, like yours, are part of the historical patchwork which define the past and perhaps point the way for future decisions.

If you would like to add anything to this pool of knowledge, or correct any errors, please visit www.habitatsandhillforts.co.uk and leave a message.

David Joyce

Captured Memories across the Hillforts of Cheshire

Other Habitats and Hillforts Publications

Key Habitat Leaflets
- 1 Species Rich Grassland.
- 2 Lowland Heath.
- 3 Broadleaf Woodlands.
- 4 Meres and Mosses.

Archaeological Leaflets
- 5 Helsby Hillfort - a late Bronze Age Cliff Top Promontory Fort.
- 6 Woodhouse Hillfort - a late Bronze Age Hill Top Enclosure.
- 7 Eddisbury Hill - a powerful Iron Age Fortress.
- 8 Kelsborrow Castle - a late Pre-historic Promontory Fort.
- 9 Beeston Crag - an important Pre-historic Hillfort Enclosure.
- 10 Maiden Castle - a complex Iron Age Cliff Edge Promontory Fort.

Circular Walk Leaflets
- 11 Helsby Hill and Woodhouse Hillfort.
- 12 Eddisbury and Kelsborrow Hillforts.
- 13 Beeston Crag.
- 14 Maiden Castle.